D0344689

Mr. Hogan, The Man I Knew

Tschetter, Kris.
Mr. Hogan, the man I
knew : an LPGA player lo
c2010.
33305222633145
cu   03/17/11

MR. HOGAN,
THE MAN I KNEW

AN LPGA PLAYER LOOKS BACK ON
AN AMAZING FRIENDSHIP AND LESSONS
SHE LEARNED FROM GOLF'S GREATEST LEGEND

KRIS TSCHETTER

with

Steve Eubanks

GOTHAM BOOKS

GOTHAM BOOKS
Published by Penguin Group (USA) Inc.
375 Hudson Street, New York, New York 10014, U.S.A.
Penguin Group (Canada), 90 Eglinton Avenue East, Suite 700, Toronto, Ontario M4P
2Y3, Canada (a division of Pearson Penguin Canada Inc.); Penguin Books Ltd, 80
Strand, London WC2R 0RL, England; Penguin Ireland, 25 St Stephen's Green, Dublin
2, Ireland (a division of Penguin Books Ltd); Penguin Group (Australia), 250 Camber-
well Road, Camberwell, Victoria 3124, Australia (a division of Pearson Australia Group
Pty Ltd); Penguin Books India Pvt Ltd, 11 Community Centre, Panchsheel Park, New
Delhi—110 017, India; Penguin Group (NZ), 67 Apollo Drive, Rosedale, North Shore
0632, New Zealand (a division of Pearson New Zealand Ltd); Penguin Books (South
Africa) (Pty) Ltd, 24 Sturdee Avenue, Rosebank, Johannesburg 2196, South Africa

Penguin Books Ltd, Registered Offices: 80 Strand, London WC2R 0RL, England

Published by Gotham Books, a member of Penguin Group (USA) Inc.

First printing, October 2010
1   3   5   7   9   10   8   6   4   2
Copyright © 2010 by Kris Tschetter and Steve Eubanks
All rights reserved

Gotham Books and the skyscraper logo are trademarks of Penguin Group (USA) Inc.
LIBRARY OF CONGRESS CATALOGING-IN-PUBLICATION DATA
has been applied for.

ISBN 978-1-592-40545-9

Printed in the United States of America
Set in ITC Galliard • Designed by Elke Sigal

Without limiting the rights under copyright reserved above, no part of this publication
may be reproduced, stored in or introduced into a retrieval system, or transmitted, in
any form, or by any means (electronic, mechanical, photocopying, recording, or otherwise), without the prior written permission of both the copyright owner and the above
publisher of this book.

The scanning, uploading, and distribution of this book via the Internet or via any other
means without the permission of the publisher is illegal and punishable by law. Please
purchase only authorized electronic editions, and do not participate in or encour-
age electronic piracy of copyrighted materials. Your support of the author's rights is
appreciated.

While the author has made every effort to provide accurate telephone numbers and
Internet addresses at the time of publication, neither the publisher nor the author as-
sumes any responsibility for errors, or for changes that occur after publication. Further,
the publisher does not have any control over and does not assume any responsibility for
author or third-party Web sites or their content.

---

*Penguin is committed to publishing works of quality and integrity.
In that spirit, we are proud to offer this book to our readers;
however, the story, the experiences, and the words
are the author's alone.*

PREFACE

When I first met Ben Hogan I knew he was a legend, I just didn't know why.

Mr. Hogan and I were as different as two people could be, and yet somehow, impossibly, we became friends. Even now, after more than two decades, I can't say, "Ben Hogan was my friend and teacher," without feeling astonishment myself and experiencing disbelief from others. I don't know which people find more difficult to believe—that Mr. Hogan would invest time in befriending me or that he was actually capable of befriending anyone. Many consider him the greatest golfer in history, and all who know the game consider him the greatest striker of the golf ball who ever lived. He is one of the rare sports icons in history who have the word *mystique* attached to their names. He was an enigma, a man so private many people thought he had died by the time we met. Most saw him as unapproachable, and when my brother and I joined Shady Oaks, where he was a member, the only strict rule we were given was to leave Mr. Hogan alone.

Every golfer who played in the "Hogan era" has a story about him, most of which involve his shunning human interaction. Those stories have been passed on, retold, and embellished over the years so that the general view of Mr. Hogan is of an aloof, insensitive man. But that was not the man I knew.

When I joined Shady Oaks Country Club as a junior member during my freshman year at Texas Christian University, I knew less about Mr. Hogan's victories than I did about his near fatal car accident that had threatened to end his career, and how he'd overcome adversity to get back to the game eleven months later. When I meet people I care more about their character and values than I do about their achievements or what they do for a living. I want to know what they think and how they feel. Some pros think that getting to know others on the course gets in the way of their focus; as for me, it puts me at ease and makes for a much more enjoyable day. I've played in countless pro-ams during my twenty-three years on tour. I like to learn how many kids my pro-am partner has and what his wife's pet peeve is about him before I find out what he does for a living. Mr. Hogan's "comeback" story is what interested me because I've always believed it's about the journey not the destination.

My dad always told me, when I would call him with yet another funny thing Mr. Hogan had said or done, that I should be writing these things down. I wish I had listened to him, because I'm sure I've forgotten more than I can remember. But as I was in the process of writing this book, I did find a journal with quite a few interesting anecdotes, such as this one from 1989.

Incredibly, I still must not have known about all his achievements.

I wrote:

I had one of my Monday lunches with Mr. Hogan today. I told him I had read the book *The Man Who Played for Glory*. (I'm not sure why I was just getting around to reading it.) I said, "You know, Mr. Hogan, I respect you and I always knew you were a great player—the greatest—but, reading that book . . . Wow! You had a lot of great years!"

Then he said, "Now wait a minute. Let's go back. Great comes from outworking them, outplaying them, and outthinking them."

Then he gave me the management talk.

That was the end of the passage, and there are a few things I find really interesting about it. The first is that after six years of knowing him I finally got around to reading a little something about him. The second was that after telling him how impressed I was, he turned the conversation away from himself and gave me another lesson. He didn't like talking about himself. He was just a supporting character in his stories.

When I think of him I remember a friend, a man who seemed anything but mysterious to me. And I am reminded of the fact that I have known for many years: I am one of the luckiest people in the world. I got the chance to know a side of Mr. Hogan that very few people ever saw.

I know this sounds unbelievable. How did a kid from South Dakota become friends with this legend she knew nothing about? There is a great line in the Kevin Costner movie *For Love of the Game.* "If you can keep your head when all about you are losing theirs, you don't understand the situation." That was me. I didn't think of him as an unapproachable legend but rather as my friend. I loved his sharp sense of humor and his compassionate heart. We would laugh and tease each other. I can hardly remember a time when I was out practicing at Shady Oaks that he didn't come out to watch or hit balls with me. One time I asked him what he'd had for lunch. When he told me he'd had bean soup with a side of bacon, I told him that was terrible for him, and that it would give him high blood pressure. "You give me high blood pressure," was his retort.

These are stories about Ben Hogan that you've never heard. I want people to finally know the funny, kind, and charitable Ben Hogan. That is who he really was. The gruff, unapproachable man was the act.

There is no question that I was in the right place at the right time. I met him toward the end of his life when he had softened. I also think he sensed I didn't want anything from him and that I was more interested in getting to know him than learning what he knew about golf. Of course along the way he did share his extraordinary knowledge of golf. I asked him about his wife and family, not how he hit a 6-iron. In fact, I can only remember one time when I asked him to come out because I needed help with something in my swing. Most of the time I just wanted his company.

He once told me he would rather be known for being a gentleman than a great golfer. He won golf tournaments for his own personal satisfaction, and he would have done so if no one were watching. Being a gentleman was what was important to him.

The incident that pushed me into finally coming forward with this tale was a televised discussion on a sports shows in which three commentators were making comparisons between Ben Hogan, Jack Nicklaus, and Tiger Woods. I was enjoying it until the subject of kids came up. Yes, the panel agreed, fatherhood would affect Tiger, but no, it shouldn't slow down his quest to break Jack's record. After all, Jack had five kids and played very well. However, the panel agreed not having children had been a good thing for Ben Hogan. "He couldn't have been as singularly focused," someone said. "He couldn't have spent all those hours on the practice tee," another chimed in. "He wouldn't have won as much," added a third.

I was so frustrated that they didn't mention how much his accident affected his career, only speculating that children would have changed it for the worse. After the crash in 1949 Mr. Hogan never again played a full schedule. In 1948, for example, he played in twenty-five tournaments, winning eleven. In 1951 he played in four tournaments and won three. He only played in three tournaments in 1952 and won one, and in 1953, the most famous year of his career, he played in a grand total of eight tournaments, winning five of them, and finishing second, third, and eighth in the other three.

I wish I could have given those journalists my opinion. I know how much Mr. Hogan loved children. He enjoyed spoiling his nieces and delighted in making funny faces at the kids playing in the Shady Oaks dining room. I have seen his sad expression when the kids he fawned over at the club would trot back to their parents. It is presumptuous to say that someone was better off not having children, especially Ben and Valerie Hogan, who adored children but were probably unable to have them.

The world deserves to know the Ben Hogan I knew, the man behind the crusty shell who spent countless afternoons helping me become a better golfer and a wiser person. It is time to eliminate the misconceptions about the man and his mystique, and to dispel the myth of Mr. Hogan as an uncaring golf machine, someone who loved golf but shunned people. It's time to tell the story of the kind, warm, generous man I was proud to call my friend.

It is time to tell the story of the Mr. Hogan I knew.

Mr. Hogan, The Man I Knew

THE UNWRITTEN RULE
AT SHADY OAKS

Like a lot of Texas stories, this one starts with a gun. Actually, I never saw a gun, but there was a desperate search for one.

It happened in 1983 at Colonial Park in Fort Worth, just a mile or so down from the TCU campus where I was a student at the time. My family is from South Dakota, which means my brothers and I grew up hitting a lot of golf balls in really bad weather. The summers are beautiful, especially around the Black Hills, but winters can be long and bitter. So when it came time for college, my brother Mike and I traveled nine hundred miles due south to Texas Christian University, a fantastic school that has great golf. I was especially thrilled to be a Horned Frog. The year I signed to play for them the women's golf team was the defending national champion. I had been a two-time Junior All-American and I had won a few junior tournaments, including the American Junior Golf Association Tournament of Champions, but to be recruited by the defending NCAA national champions was an honor and a thrill. The fact that Mike had already been there two years might have had something to do with my being offered a spot on the TCU team. I thanked my lucky stars every day that I was in Fort Worth, especially in April when I was wearing shorts instead of my rain suit on the golf course. Throw in the fact that once a week the team got to play at Colonial Country Club, one of the greatest golf courses in America, and I couldn't wait to trade in my ice skates for a pair of golf shoes.

Even in the Dakotas we knew about Colonial. It's a classic club, founded in 1936, and it hosted the U.S. Open five years later. In 1946 the members put on the first Colonial National Invitational, one of the most popular weeks on the PGA Tour. Today that tournament is the longest-running event other than the Masters to be held at the same course. I loved Colonial from the first moment I saw it. The old-style design suited my game, and I knew I would improve by playing there. Plus, it was impossible not to get a thrill when you walked past the Wall of Champions, an area by the first tee set up to honor those who have won at Colonial. Craig Wood, "the Blond Bomber," is up there for winning the 1941 U.S. Open. Then there are the invitational winners: a Hall of Fame

Who's Who that includes Arnold Palmer, Jack Nicklaus, Lee Trevino, Billy Casper, Sam Snead, and Ben Crenshaw. But the name that stands out is Ben Hogan, if for no other reason than that he's on the wall five times. Mr. Hogan won the first Colonial National Invitational and then followed up with a win in the tournament's second year. He won it once more in 1953 and made back-to-back wins for a second time in 1954. In 1959 he won the invitational for an unprecedented fifth time. It was his sixty-fourth career win, and his last.

By the time I got there, the course had been called "Hogan's Alley" for so long that nobody could remember who hung the nickname on it. No one disputed that Mr. Hogan's presence could be felt throughout every square inch of the club. He and Colonial's founder, a local businessman named Marvin Leonard, were longtime friends and business partners. In fact, Mr. Leonard had financially backed Mr. Hogan during his early days on tour. Mr. Hogan had returned the favor by being a loyal friend and fierce advocate for the club and its tournament for decades. He would show up for the Champions Dinner wearing the red plaid jacket given to the winner. Far from being the cold, steely eyed "Hawk" the media had portrayed, Mr. Hogan was the perfect party host, telling stories and making all the past champions feel welcome.

When I first arrived in Fort Worth I knew some of that history but not much. As a teenager I was never interested in the history of the game. All I knew was that playing Colonial was one of the coolest things about being at TCU. Our team also got to play Ridglea Country Club, a thirty-six-hole Jay Morrish–design that opened in the late fifties, and Rivercrest Country Club, one of the oldest clubs in Texas, founded in 1911. All were great.

Ridglea and Rivercrest didn't have the best practice facilites, so other than the one day a week we played at Colonial I didn't have access to a club where I could spend hours working on my game. That was okay. I had no problem taking my own shag bag out to Colonial Park, a public park tucked between a busy road and Colonial Country Club, with a few towering oak trees and open space for picnics. It was actually more convenient, and because it was quiet and different, it was more fun. At least it was until the moment a strange woman walked up and asked me for a gun.

As usual nobody else was around. The area I had chosen as my makeshift range sat across the road from the fourth green at Colonial and was almost always deserted. That was one of the reasons I loved it so much. This was the pre-iPod age, so I would open the doors and trunk of my car and hit balls for as long as I wanted with my stereo blasting the latest from Bruce Springsteen, REO Speedwagon, and of course Michael Jackson's *Thriller*, which turned out to be a perfect soundtrack for the day's events.

I had been practicing a couple of hours when the woman appeared out of nowhere. I didn't see her until she was right next to me. She startled me when she said, "Excuse me."

"Hi," I said.

She looked around nervously and said, "I don't mean to bother you, but do you have a gun?"

I'm not sure what I expected after "Excuse me," but "Do you have a gun?" was well down the list. I don't think I even processed the question. I just automatically answered, "No, I'm sorry, I don't."

Then came the story: "Do you see that truck over there?" she said.

In Texas "Do you see that truck?" is like saying, "Do you see that bird?" in an aviary. But there weren't many vehicles nearby, and I did, indeed, see the pickup in question.

"That man has been following me all day," she continued. "I don't know who he is, but I'm scared."

I could have said, *Sorry, I'd love to help, but I'm working on a knockdown cut right now.* But I said what all good South Dakotans would say: "Get in my car. I'll take you where you need to go."

I've done plenty of things in my life that weren't safe, like the time I ran out of gas on my way to the airport in Tucson. I had missed the cut in Phoenix and was trying to catch a flight to Nashville to watch the basketball game between Belmont University and its biggest rival, Lipscomb University. My friend Rick Byrd coached the undefeated Belmont team and it was their last game of the season. I had friends in Nashville and going there sounded like a lot more fun than watching my peers play on the weekend. Unfortunately, I didn't look at the gas gauge until the car started sputtering. Nothing screams "bad move" quite like standing outside of a rental car in the middle of the desert. Thankfully, a man in a truck pulling a horse trailer stopped and asked if I needed help. He could have been one of the crazies out there for all I knew, but when all you can see are cacti and scorpions, and your flight is leaving in a little over an hour, you take what you can get. I hopped in his truck and rode to the nearest gas station. He actually turned out to be a very nice guy. He took me back to my car and even helped me fill the tank. I thanked him and told him I would leave him tickets for the tournament the following week.

Then there was the time when ten of us went to dinner after the final round of a tournament. People were catching rides, and some guy named Steve asked if I would drive him to the restaurant. I wasn't sure who he was, but it was one of those dinners where some people didn't know each other, but everybody knew somebody, so I gave Steve a lift and we had a nice chat. I had played well that week, so I bought dinner. The next day some of us began talking and we realized that Steve didn't know anybody and nobody knew him. He was the perfect party crasher. He'd tagged along, got a free meal, and got away with it.

None of those incidents would register as high on the danger meter as giving a ride to a stranger who had just asked for a gun. What could possibly go wrong?

Thankfully, everything worked out for the best. I dropped the woman at her house not too far away and made sure we weren't followed. She thanked me and I went out for a quick nine holes. Later that day I went over to my brother's apartment to tell him what had happened.

"You did what?" he yelled.

"Well, I couldn't just leave her there," I said.

During the stern big brother lecture he stopped suddenly as if something had dawned on him and broke out laughing. "This is perfect. You have to call Mom and Dad and tell them what happened."

"Why?" I asked. I didn't want to worry our parents.

"Because when they realize this happened at Colonial Park and you were out there because you had nowhere else to practice, they'll spring for those junior memberships at Shady Oaks."

Mike was already thinking three steps ahead. In ninety seconds he had gotten over the shock of my story and realized that my giving a ride to a stranger in search of a gun would scare our parents into springing for memberships at a club with a fantastic practice area. And not just any club, but Shady Oaks, one of the best in Texas. With a small, golf-loving membership and a great Robert Trent Jones–designed course, Shady Oaks is considered the "player's club" of Fort Worth. All the serious golfers in town eventually find their way out there. That was how the club got started. Once Colonial became popular and crowded, Marvin Leonard, who owned a chain of retail stores as well as a healthy number of oil contracts in the area, built Shady Oaks for a golf-centered group of his friends. His first member was Ben Hogan.

Shady Oaks stayed loyal to Mr. Leonard's vision long after he was gone, although they did occasionally open the doors to new junior members. My gun incident occurred right in the middle of one of those membership drives. The hard part wasn't the initiation fee—that was only $750—it was getting in. Like a lot of exclusive clubs, Shady was very selective about whom they invited. Fortunately, my father knew a member who could put in a nice word if Dad would give us the go-ahead. It made perfect sense, or at least Mike thought so. We needed a good place to practice, and the "Do you have a gun?" story could be just the thing to push Dad over to our side.

It worked like a charm. I hadn't finished the story when my father said, "That's it. We're getting you those memberships at Shady Oaks."

A couple of weeks later, Mike and I entered the clubhouse as new members.

The place was surprisingly informal to be so exclusive. As far as I could tell, there were very few rules at Shady Oaks. There were no tee times and there was no limit to the size of your group, as long as you kept pace. There weren't just foursomes at Shady, there were "gangsomes." It was said that the gamblers didn't trust one another enough to play in separate groups, so they played together in their own carts. I still remember how funny it looked to see eight or nine carts come flying down the hill. They would get to their balls and hit with very little time between shots and they always played in less than four hours. The only written rule was "Men must wear shirts." The joke was that tops were optional for women. There were some unwritten rules, though. The one impressed upon us most emphatically was that you did not bother Mr. Hogan.

"If he wants to talk to you, he will talk to you," the general manager said as he was giving Mike and me the nickel tour of our new club. The message was clear: We were not to initiate contact.

Every serious golfer knew at least one Ben Hogan story. The tale every kid heard growing up was that "Ben Hogan hit balls until his hands bled." That vivid imagery of a tireless work ethic was seared into my brain, as were many of the less flattering tales of his antisocial behavior. I'd heard that Arnold Palmer didn't care for him very much. I'm told that according to Arnie's version of events, at the 1958 Masters Arnie had asked Mr. Hogan if he could play a practice round with him early in the week. Mr. Hogan said yes, and they played with Dow Finsterwald and Jimmy Demaret. Arnie missed some fairways as he often did. In his memory of the day when they finished their round, Finsterwald and Demaret sat at a table in the dining room with Mr. Hogan, but Arnie wasn't invited to join them, which he took as a slight. Then, during lunch, he overheard Mr. Hogan ask Demaret, "So, that kid we played with today, Palmer, how'd he get into the Masters?" Years later, I would come to realize that even if every word of that story occurred exactly as Arnie remembered it, Mr. Hogan meant no harm. He would have assumed that Arnie would join them for lunch without being invited. Extending a special invitation to sit down at the table would seem unnecessary. Also, I'm sure he was curious how a player he did not know had qualified for the Masters. It might have come across as an insult, but knowing Mr. Hogan I'm sure it wasn't intentional. Mr. Hogan once told me he thought Arnie was a "nice young fellow," which was great praise coming from Mr. Hogan. I remember thinking at the time, *Isn't Mr. Palmer in his mid-fifties?*

When we first joined Shady Oaks I only knew the Ben Hogan of legend. I knew he made great clubs. His were the first new clubs I had ever owned. Dad finally broke down and got me a new set after two of the clubheads flew off my hand-me-down irons while I was hitting on the range. I'd skimmed through *Five Lessons: The Modern Fundamentals of Golf,* Mr. Hogan's classic instructional book, which remains the best-selling golf book of all time. In fact, one of the hottest players in the game at that time, Larry Nelson, had never hit a golf ball until he was in his early twenties and out of the army; however, he learned the fundamentals well enough to win three major championships by simply studying Mr. Hogan's book.

Of course, anyone with a passing interest in the game

knew that Mr. Hogan was the greatest ball-striker who ever played. He had succeeded in digging the most consistent golf swing in history out of nothing but desire and daylight. He had willed himself to greatness through sweat and an unbelievably determined spirit.

Then, of course, there was the car crash that almost killed him.

It happened on Groundhog Day, February 2, 1949, as he and Valerie were driving from El Paso back home to Fort Worth. An icy road and a Greyhound bus in the wrong lane led to a head-on collision. The only thing that saved Mr. Hogan's life was his last-second attempt to protect Valerie by throwing his body in front of hers. Photos of the mangled car left everyone wondering how anybody got out alive. Mr. Hogan's legs were crushed, and he suffered head trauma that affected his eyesight for the rest of his life. He was told he might never walk again, and he would certainly never play golf again. His comeback win at the U.S. Open sixteen months later was the stuff of movie legend. In fact, even before he won that Open at Merion, a movie had been made about his life: *Follow the Sun*, starring Glenn Ford. He didn't say what he thought of the movie, but he did say that Glenn Ford couldn't make himself look like a golfer throwing up grass to check the wind.

Those were the only things I knew about Mr. Hogan at the time, other than that he was a founding member at Shady Oaks and one of the few who came to the club every day.

What I didn't fully appreciate at the time was the giant shadow that he cast. I had little appreciation for the spell he held over people in golf and the reverential distance everyone felt they needed to keep from him. I was six when Mr. Hogan played in his last golf tournament, and while I appreciated the things he had done in the game, I hadn't taken time to understand the full measure of the man. To me he was a black-and-white figure in old news clippings, a pencil sketch in an instruction book, a champion who was more known among my generation for the golf clubs his company made than for the tournaments he'd won. Thankfully, I was playing Hogan clubs when I became a member at Shady Oaks, so at least I didn't have to worry about offending him with my equipment.

The first few times Mike and I went to practice and play at Shady Oaks, we would hang around in the clubhouse a few extra minutes checking out every old man who walked by. Most of them wore front-clipped touring caps, the kind of hats that had become so synonymous with Mr. Hogan that they were commonly known as "Hogan hats." *Is that him? No. How 'bout that guy over there?* We weren't sure we would recognize Mr. Hogan when we saw him. When I did finally see him for the first time as he was walking out of the pro shop, I realized that he would have been impossible to miss. Years had weathered him, but the eyes, the high cheekbones, the strong hands, and even stronger forearms were unmistakable. Anyone who had seen a photo or clip of Mr. Hogan would have recognized him immediately. Even a non-golfer, someone who wouldn't know Ben Hogan from Babe Ruth, would have recognized from his carriage that this man had a presence about him that was unmistakable.

The first few times our paths crossed, I turned around and acted as if I hadn't seen him. *My, my, this plaque on the wall is interesting. So, Mr. Summers had a hole-in-one in 1977. Isn't that something.* Then one day I said to myself: *This is crazy. I say hello to every other man out here. I'm not going to treat him any differently. I'm not being true to myself and I'm being rude to him. He can like it or not, but I'm just going be me.*

The next day when Mr. Hogan walked by, I said hi. He smiled, and replied with a friendly hello and walked on. He was carrying his 6-iron and three balls, his standard routine. By the time Mike and I became members at Shady Oaks, Mr. Hogan didn't officially "practice" anymore. He would grab a club and three balls and go for walks on the short course or "Little Nine," as it was known. "Just getting a little exercise," he would say.

When he walked back into the clubhouse that first day after I had spoken to him, I was still practicing. He looked at me, smiled again, and said, "You're still here? Keep working at it."

I didn't realize it, but that brief interaction would be the start of a long friendship with one of the greatest champions of all time, a man I grew to admire and love. It didn't seem like much at the time, just a kind old member being nice to a kid, but at that moment my young golfing life changed forever.

"HIT A FEW HUNDRED LIKE THAT, AND YOU'LL GET IT."

I think it was my love of practice that caught his eye. Mr. Hogan was the godfather of all driving range rats. During his prime, he would hit five hundred balls every morning, and if things didn't go exactly as he'd planned, he would hit another five hundred in the afternoon. Sometimes he worked from sunup until sundown on one club or one shot until he felt he had mastered it. In his heyday, his routine included a hearty breakfast followed by a trip to the range where he would begin his practice session. If he didn't have a particular shot in mind, he would hit fifty balls with every club in his bag. Then he would break for lunch, usually a white bread sandwich or a bowl of soup, the kind of austere rations that many from his generation considered a feast no matter how successful they later became. Afterward, he would either play or return to the range for another fifty ball per club session. Hitting good shots was not enough for him. He would often work for a day, week, or sometimes longer on controlling trajectory and spin with one club.

My practices weren't that regimented or obsessive, but I did spend a lot of time hitting balls and chipping and putting. Practice had always been one of my favorite activities, going back to my childhood. Our pro growing up in South Dakota, Terry Crouch, was well ahead of his time in his support of junior golf. We had full use of the practice facilities, and if there was an open tee time, we were free to go. We knew we had to keep up and follow the rules, but we played and practiced as much as we wanted and he gave that same opportunity to the kids who worked for him. He was my first teacher and gave me a great foundation.

My parents were also supportive. They introduced us to the game, gave us the tools we needed to succeed, and then were wise enough to let us be independent and learn to love golf on our own. My father was one of the only ophthalmologists in Sioux Falls when we were growing up. He worked hard at his practice and hard at his golf game. He was always busy, so Mom took us to most tournaments. Both she and Dad remained at arm's length until we needed them. Then they leapt in to help. At one point some old-timers in South Dakota wanted to ban juniors from the Men's and Women's

State Championships. My mother would have none of that. She went on a crusade to see that the South Dakota amateur championships remained opened to any resident who qualified, regardless of age. Looking back, the sacrifices she made for us to play golf were extraordinary. I'm able to appreciate now that Mom might have enjoyed a week away with her friends instead of carting us to this or that tournament, but she never complained. My brothers, Mike and Eric, and I always came first.

There were two things that moved my early golf career along. The first was that as an afterthought my parents entered me in the Junior World tournament out in San Diego. Mike was the serious golfer and they were taking him to play. When they found out there was a ten-and-under age group for girls, they asked me if I wanted to play as well. I played with Heather Farr in the final round and ended up finishing second to Karen Nicoletti. I came home with a trophy and spent the next couple of weeks accepting the praise of members and friends. I think, at the time, I enjoyed the praise and congratulations more than I did the golf, but that tournament revved up my early enthusiasm for the game.

That enthusiasm would have probably lasted as long as the average ten-year-old's attention span if I hadn't had a friend to join me. I was fortunate that another girl my age named Nancy Steen played. She loved golf as much as I did, and we played every day in the summers, alternating our time between the golf course, range, and the swimming pool. Nancy's father, Ike, played with my dad in his Saturday-morning game. We caddied every week, even though we probably drove them a little crazy. We were always lagging behind with our pull-carts and complaining, but we saw our fathers gambling and having a great time. Caddying fueled our interest and also introduced me to my lifelong habit of gambling on the golf course.

I remember my first year on tour my dad said, "You need to find some friends who will gamble with you. Don't any of those girls gamble out there?"

I told him Cindy Rarick did but I wasn't sure she would let me in her game.

Dad laughed hard and said, "She's about tenth on the money list and you're a hundred and fortieth. I think she'll let you play." He was right, and to this day, Cindy and I are great friends and are known for our gambling games during practice. At one event, we played our regular nassau during our practice round. Afterward we had a closest-to-the-hole wedge contest, and then we played our favorite five point chipping game, and a few putting games. When we finally wore ourselves out and were ready to go home, I said, "Cindy, do you realize we've played all day long and we ended up dead even? How is that possible?"

"I don't know, Tschetter," she said. "But we better play one more game."

Most people who put in "Hoganesque" hours on the

practice tee don't mind the solitude. For a golfer there was no better way to get lost inside yourself than to head to the range with a mountain of balls at your side. This is the equivalent of a DO NOT DISTURB sign. A player goes to the practice area to work on his swing, and at a certain skill level, working on the swing requires almost a transcendental level of focus. When he was younger, Justin Leonard used to get so lost in his practice sessions that he lost track of time. Then his hands would start shaking and he would realize that he'd been on the range for nine hours and had forgotten to eat. Colin Montgomerie was once practicing at a European Tour event, during which a friend watched him on the range for close to two hours. At one point Monty nodded and said hi to his friend, but a day later Montgomerie saw his friend again and said, "Hey, I didn't realize you were coming out this week." When the friend said, "Colin, you spoke to me on the range yesterday. I watched you for more than an hour," Monty had no recollection of the event.

That has happened to me while playing in tournaments. I have had conversations with people between holes and then seen them at the end of the day and not remembered having talked. Sometimes I'm on autopilot during a round, but the practice tee is different. I'm much more relaxed when I practice. For as long as I can remember I've listened to music while practicing. It actually helps me stay focused. Prior to digital playlists, I would make practice tapes of my favorite music.

A putting tape might consist of James Taylor, Billy Joel, and Amy Grant, while my driver tape was more upbeat—anything from John Mellencamp to Meat Loaf.

As different as our routines might have been, Mr. Hogan noticed my devotion to the practice tee. Not long after Mike and I joined Shady Oaks, I became friends with Judy, the wife of a member named Bob Wynn. He was a frequent lunch guest at Mr. Hogan's table, so he mentioned me to Mr. Hogan. "You should go look at her," Bob said. Mr. Hogan answered with a grunt, his typical response to those kinds of suggestions. But he noticed.

We had continued to say "Good afternoon" and "See you later" to each other as we passed. Those encounters became easier each time, although I was still a little uneasy because everyone I knew kept telling me I should be. They kept telling me tales of a curt, cold man who wanted to be left alone. He didn't seem to be like that at all, in fact he smiled and spoke every time I saw him, but that was only in passing.

I had no idea he had taken an interest in me until he walked up to me one day while I was practicing on the last hole of the Little Nine, and our conversation immediately went well beyond the normal hello. The Little Nine was the perfect place to practice because you could find all the different lies and conditions that you would experience on the course. If you needed to work on uphill approaches with a helping left-to-right wind, there was a spot near the creek for that. If you wanted to hit drivers into a hurting right-to-left wind, there was a spot at the top of the hill between the 18th tee and 11th green of the big course where you could spend all day working on that shot. I went there because I felt that hitting my own balls and having to retrieve them afterward made me focus harder on each shot. It is easy on the driving range to spray one shot left and the next shot right; you just raked over another ball from the pile without worrying about where the last one ended up. When I had to go retrieve them, I tried really hard to keep all my shots in close proximity. Plus, I could listen to my music and not bother anyone. On this day I was working on pitch shots from a tight lie to a slightly elevated green.

When he saw me he suggested, "Try really weakening your hands."

I was so stunned that he had said something other than hello, and that the first words out of his mouth were a suggestion about something to do with my grip that I froze. I was like a kid going into brain lock when Santa asked what you wanted for Christmas. Mr. Hogan had just given me a golf tip! Wow! But what did he mean by really weaken my hands?

"Weaken them. Left hand under, right hand over," he said.

Rather than try to talk me through it (something that was never his strong suit), he took my hands in his and rotated them the way he wanted them with both thumbs on the left side of the grip (or counterclockwise). His hands were large and strong and rough, especially for a man in his seventies, but they were also exacting. He knew right where to place my hands on the golf club to get the desired result.

"Hit a few hundred like that, and you'll get it," he said. And he was off, back to his walk.

At first I was afraid to take my hands off the club because I wasn't sure I could get them back on exactly as Mr. Hogan wanted them. Then I realized I just had to weaken them as much as I possibly could, and they would be in the same place. It wasn't a shot I would use often, but it was a shot to tuck away in my arsenal and bring out when needed. After hitting several shots I realized that this grip forced my elbows closer together, a fundamental that Mr. Hogan always preached. It also forced me to swing the club with the big muscles in my shoulders and torso. With the grip he showed me, I could quiet my hands and wrists when hitting short pitches. It made it so easy to loft the ball and land it softly. Later I would realize while practicing with this grip that it was the cure for mistakes I had always struggled with in my swing. And it took Mr. Hogan less than a minute to show me and be on his way. It was the first of what would turn out to be many enlightening sessions we had together.

The next day I was on the Little Nine hitting shots just short of the 9th green. This time I was working on hitting 7-iron shots off a sidehill lie.

Mr. Hogan was out once again for what most people would have characterized as an afternoon walk. He didn't practice at the time, but he did stroll around the grounds with a 6-iron in his hand and three balls in his pocket. Most of the time the club was a walking stick, but he would occasionally throw the balls down and hit a few. He never appeared to be working on anything. He looked like a man who hit a few balls because he needed an excuse to stay outside a little longer. This day he walked up to where I was practicing and said, "How are you hitting them?"

This is golf's version of "How you doing?"—a rhetorical question that isn't meant to be answered honestly or specifically. The only acceptable response is "Good," or "Fine." But this was Ben Hogan. I wasn't about to let a moment like this pass, so I said, "Actually, I'm having a little trouble keeping these 7-irons from going left off this sidehill lie."

His walk came to sudden halt. He stared at me with those piercing eyes for several seconds. Then he said, "Let's see."

"I'm sorry?" I said, unsure exactly what he meant.

He nodded toward the balls I had scattered on the ground. "Hit one and let me see," he said.

Then it dawned on me that Ben Hogan was about to critique my full swing. I was so conditioned to be afraid of him, but youth and ignorance kept me from being paralyzed. He looked like a nice enough old man. What could it hurt to have him watch me hit a few?

Once again he focused on my hands. That should have come as no surprise. Mr. Hogan had a simple philosophy when it came to golf: The player's only contact with the ball comes through the club, and the only contact with the club comes through the hands. To him the hands are like tires touching a racetrack. The engine, transmission, steering, and aerodynamics don't mean a thing, if the only parts of the car touching the road are faulty. In golf, everything begins with the hands, and Mr. Hogan knew more about the effects of the grip on the swing than anyone who had ever played. According to Mr. Hogan, the slightest variation in any aspect of the hands, whether it was the position of the thumb or an increase in the pressure of one finger, could change the swing entirely.

One of the greatest stories in the game is Mr. Hogan's self-imposed hiatus, when he tried to come up with a cure for his terrible hook. "I was an awful player," he said of that period. His nemesis was a hard-slinging right-to-lefter or, as he called it, "the terror of the field mice." After two failed attempts on tour, he went home and vowed to give up the game if he couldn't come up with a way to cure that shot. He would later tell his friends, "It's not the hook that kills you; it's the fear of hitting it."

My dad was always telling me I needed to hit fades. One of his favorite sayings is: "You can talk to a fade but a hook won't listen." I think young players today don't even know what a duck hook is. It is much harder to hit with the newer balls and advanced equipment. Twenty-year-olds swing away with drivers now, never thinking about the possibility of a low, left, smothered hook. I often stand on the tee with a utility iron in my hand watching a young player pull out a driver, and I think, *Don't they see that trouble left?* Then it dawns on me that if you've never swung a wood that was actually made of wood, or hit a ball that would spin hard in both directions, you have no idea. For those of us who learned to play pre-1990, the duck hook is imprinted on our souls.

Not knowing if the next tee shot would be a hard-left nosedive kept Mr. Hogan on the defensive and out of the winner's circle. As he often did, when he needed to make a change, he started with his hands. By weakening his left hand, turning it to the left until he could only see one knuckle of his left hand, and then feeling the clubface rotate open on the way back, he realized that he could hit the ball hard and it would not go left. "With that grip, I knew I could hit the ball as hard as I wanted to with my right hand and it would produce a slight fade. That was a great feeling!"

He focused on his grip for the rest of his career as well as how his grips were put on his clubs. He had a reminder turned to five o'clock on all of his full cord grips. A reminder is a ridge on the inside of a grip that goes down the back of the club. Turning it to five o'clock helped him feel comfortable with the fade grip and also allowed him to be exacting when he put his hands on the club. Every pre-shot routine began with him holding the club up like a standard-bearer holding a flag. It wasn't until he had methodically gone through the mechanics of his grip, examining his hands and making them perfect, that he went into his setup and hit the shot. Even during rounds, he would walk down the fairway holding a club aloft so he could inspect his grip. Every shot started with the hands for him, and every kind of shot could be created through nuanced adjustments to the grip. He especially preached weaker hands for little chips and pitches. He felt that this gave him much more control.

In the first of our many full-swing sessions, it didn't take long for Mr. Hogan to get right to the point. "What are you doing with your hands on the club like that?" he asked.

I couldn't have dropped the club any faster if it had been a hot frying pan. "What do you mean?"

He had me hold the club again and insisted that my left-hand grip was too strong. "You should only see one knuckle on the left hand." Indeed my left thumb was on the right side of the grip instead of straight down the center as he'd advocated in his book.

I'd always had a strong grip, in part because my joints are so loose that my thumb would dislocate at the top of my swing if I didn't brace it in there at address. But also, like a lot of kids who started playing golf at a young age, I grooved a strong left-hand grip because it made it easier to swing a club that was too heavy. Throughout my career, no one had been successful in getting me to weaken my grip. That was fine when I was ten but when I was twenty, that grip caused me to hit more than a few hooks.

Mr. Hogan went into incredible detail talking about what part of my left thumb was on the grip, something that had never crossed my mind. It was like thinking about what part of your fingers touched a pencil. I'd never given a moment's thought to the way I placed my thumb on the grip, but Mr. Hogan had. He said that instead of putting the fat part of my thumb on the grip, I needed to put the pressure on the left side of the left thumb (something I was never able to achieve). He would meticulously put my hands on the club starting by putting the middle knuckle of my left index finger on the grip and working it at an angle until the top of the grip sat below the heel of my left hand. He believed that the three bottom fingers of the left hand and the middle fingers of the right hand were the most important fingers for the grip. "You can't hook it with a weak grip and where you put that left thumb is important," he said. "Once you get your hands on the club properly all you have to do is swing."

It seemed so strange to me. No one had ever focused so much on my hands. I hit a few without success. He still wasn't happy with my grip. (It eventually got better but it was never to his liking.) Then I thought, *Oh, what the heck,* and said, "Why don't you show me?"

He shook his head and said, "No, no, you keep hitting them. You'll get it."

"I need to see it," I said. "Show me what you mean so I'll understand."

Looking back, I can only shake my head at the audacity of telling Ben Hogan to hit a shot for me. I'm not sure why I wasn't intimidated. Here I was, a teenager asking Ben Hogan to hit a few shots so I could get an idea of what he was trying to teach me. I remember thinking that I really wanted to see him hit one up close and personal. He kept saying no, but I can be very persuasive.

I think that's when he figured out I wasn't afraid of him, and I was going to keep pestering him until he did what I asked. Finally, he reached into his pocket and dropped the three balls. Then I watched as he slipped his hands around the grip of his 6-iron, checking the position of his left thumb before folding his right hand on top. It just looked like his hands were home, like that was where they were meant to be. Even though the body was older and a tad plumper than the photos and drawings I'd seen, the setup was the same. His knees, hips, arms, and shoulders were open to his very closed feet. He planted his right foot perfectly square to the line with his left foot splayed at exactly forty-five degrees. *How did he do it every time?* The back was straight and the left hip high, just as they had been in his prime. Then he whipped the club back knee-high in his patented waggle, kicked his right knee in to trigger his swing, and POW! Like the crack of a bullwhip, the quick, slashing swing sent a ball soaring toward his target.

He repeated the process. The second swing was a carbon copy of the first, as was the result, a soft 6-iron shot that landed softly on the green. His third swing was just like the previous two, again with similar results. I had been hitting 7-iron shots short of the green. He hit three 6-irons to what looked like about ten feet of the pin. With that, he looked at me with a little smile and said, "Keep working at it," and walked off to retrieve his balls, the 6-iron becoming a cane once more.

I still didn't understand everything he was trying to get me to do with my hands. In fact, as I stood there watching him walk away, only one word came to mind: *Wow.*

These were the first of many sessions we had together. Most of them weren't lessons in the traditional sense, because Mr. Hogan wasn't a classic teacher. He demonstrated better than he explained and he was a tinkerer. If something worked, he kept it and honed it. If something didn't work, he discarded it quickly and moved on to something different. He would always say, "Try this. If it doesn't work, throw it away." He could only tell me what to feel. He might try to get me to understand something by saying it five different ways. But he understood that not everything worked for everybody. And while he knew more about the golf swing than anyone who ever lived, he wasn't always the best at explaining what he meant.

He was very careful when he spoke. He thought everything through before he would say anthing. You would ask him a question and he might not answer for a minute or two (at least it felt that long). He would just stare at you while he was formulating his answer. Not prone to wasting words, he was making sure he gave you his best answer possible—his definitive answer. I eventually got used to it, but it made me uncomfortable in the early days of our friendship.

The members would later warn me to be careful about taking lessons from Mr. Hogan. According to more than a few sources, certain people Mr. Hogan had "helped" either couldn't physically do the things he'd wanted or had overdone the drills he'd given them to the point where their games suffered and they never recovered. That was probably true, especially for those he only watched once or twice. But he watched me every day. He devoted his full attention to me, and I had an all-access pass to his knowledge.

As a carefree kid, I used to take a big yellow boom box onto the Little Nine so I could listen to music while I practiced. Then, when Mr. Hogan showed up, I would discreetly slip over and turn the volume down. Shady Oaks was a relaxed place. One of the things I loved about it was that you could wear jeans anytime, anywhere. I don't know why, but I loved hitting balls in jeans. Maybe it was because I viewed it as forbidden. There aren't many clubs that allow jeans. I look back on those days now, hitting balls in jeans with Mr. Hogan while listening to the Go-Go's and Jackson Browne, and wonder, with a big smile, *What was I thinking?*

My youthful idiosyncrasies never seemed to bother him much. My grip was another story. He was never happy with how I put my hands on the club. I was born with hypermobility due to Ehlers-Danlos syndrome, or EDS. That means I have loose joints, which may sound like a good thing, but mine are too loose and it affects almost every joint in my body. People with EDS lack collagen, which is a protein found in connective tissue. My tendons and ligaments are so lax that they don't do the job of supporting my joints. So basically, the only things working for me are my muscles. That is why my thumb would collapse at the top of my backswing if I didn't brace it in at address. The fact that my left thumb would dislocate at times frustrated him as much as it did me. But he kept at it, turning my left hand into a weaker position than I was accustomed to, until we compromised on something resembling a neutral left-hand grip. Then he meticulously put my right hand on the club, taking it into his weathered, calloused hands, wrapping one finger at a time around the grip. He made sure the handle rested just below the second joint of the middle two fingers of my right hand, and then he gently folded my hand around until my index finger was on the club like a trigger on a gun.

The first day we worked on it, it felt like my left hand was tied underneath the club with a bandage. My first swing, I hit about three inches behind the ball. It flew thirty yards right of my target and landed forty yards short. My first thought was *I just hit a fat push in front of Ben Hogan. Where is the nearest hole I can crawl into?*

"That's better," he said.

"Better than what?"

"Better than that other thing you were doing."

Then he was quiet. I hit another shot, and then another and another until the grip started to feel semi-comfortable and I started making better contact. Twenty or so balls into the session, he said, "Good."

That was that. Lesson over. He watched a few more and then went to practice at his favorite spot.

At some point I stopped thinking that having him out with me was unusual. It became our routine. I would get out to the course sometime after noon. I parked on the golf shop side of the clubhouse so I could get a cart and load my clubs. Then I would ride to the grill and get something to drink. If he was sitting at his usual table in the men's grill, he would come outside and say hello, or I might stick my head around the corner and say hi to him. Other times I might just wave as I drove by and not long afterward he would be on the Little Nine with me. Sometimes he would drive by and throw me a Snickers bar on his way to his favorite spot. I would hear him say, "Here's your lunch," as he was driving away. Other times he would stop and watch me hit before he went on to practice. At some point, we just started practicing together. I hit most of the balls, but I was more than happy to sit and watch him hit when he was in the mood. Imagine: Hogan SyberVision.

In addition to getting a front-row seat to a long-running Ben Hogan ball-striking clinic, I also got to know the man, and realized that he had a great wit and a dry sense of humor. We would banter and laugh. Once, after I hit a shot fat, I said, "Oh, I chunked it."

"You what?" he said.

"I chunked it."

"What's that?"

"I hit it fat," I said.

"Well, why didn't you just say so?"

"You mean you've never heard anyone say 'I chunked' a shot?" I said. "Am I going to have to translate for you?"

He answered with "I guess you are."

Another time I showed up at the Hogan factory wearing blue pants and a blue sweater. He took one look at me and said, "What, you couldn't find anything blue to wear today?"

That is the kind of banter friends expect from each other on the golf course. In hindsight, the fact that Mr. Hogan had it with me is surprising, but at the time I thought nothing of it. Early on I wondered how long he would continue to come out and watch me hit balls. I had no idea then that the answer would be: the rest of his life.

. . .

Before long, it became unusual for him not to make an appearance on the Little Nine with me. Each time, he would check my grip, just as he checked his own throughout his playing career. The more I listened to his comments about the role of the hands, the more I realized he was right. As the weaker grip became more comfortable, I found I could swing the club freely through the hitting area without worrying about hooking it.

"Once you get that grip mastered, you can go at it as hard as you want," he said. "Fire that right hand." He wanted my thumb and index finger of my right hand to steady the club while the two middle fingers produced the power.

I hit a shot as hard as I thought I could.

"That wasn't hard," he shot back, shaking his head like I'd just done something terrible. "Hit it hard!"

I took another hard, fast swing, the kind of thrash that would have normally produced a screaming hook. He didn't say anything, so I assumed it was better. I also realized that he was right, no matter how hard I went after it, the ball would not go left.

"That's the article I'm going to write," he said.

"What's that?" I asked.

"The left hand is the steering wheel and the right hand is the gas. Once you get your grip on there correctly, the left hand controls where the ball goes, and the right hand provides the power."

"When are you going to write that article?" I asked.

He smiled slightly and said, "Someday."

He also told me that he'd always believed that if the club traveled faster after impact than before impact, the ball would fly farther and straighter. "I know I saw that once in a physics book." He said, "It said that if an object that hit another object was traveling faster after impact, the object being hit would travel farther and straighter. See if you can find me that book. Would you please?"

Physics isn't really my thing, so it took me a while but I did finally find it for him. The book had an entire chapter devoted to acceleration and the effects an accelerating object has when striking an object at rest. He read it and gave me back the book looking satisfied. "I knew I'd seen that somewhere," he said. "Thank you for bringing it to me."

It didn't take long for me to realize that it made no difference to Mr. Hogan that I was a woman. He thought Mickey Wright had the best swing in golf. Gender didn't modify his belief in the fundamentals of the game. He believed that anyone, man or woman, could learn to hit a golf ball correctly if they adhered to the basic fundamentals.

It wasn't until much later that I realized I was giving him something in return for the help he offered me. I got him away from the table in the men's grill and out on the course with me for at least a couple of hours every day. By the mid-eighties, before we met, Mr. Hogan's golf swing hadn't changed, but his enthusiasm had waned. He still went to the office every day, but his business, the Ben Hogan Company, was being run by others. Many of his friends were gone. Marvin Leonard died in 1970. In December of 1983, his friend and fellow Texan Jimmy Demaret died of a heart attack while getting out of a golf cart. Claude Harmon, a man Mr. Hogan called "one of the best friends I ever had," passed away in a Houston hospital in 1989, but arthritis had kept him away from the game for years. By the time he and I became friends, Mr. Hogan never hit more balls than he could carry in his pocket, and if anyone was around, he wouldn't even take a swing.

I'm not sure what got him back into practicing. Maybe it was just that he got a little taste of it again and the old desire came back. I remember watching him hit five woods one day. They were in a very tight circle. "Mr. Hogan," I said, "that is a pretty good pattern."

He stopped, turned, and pinned me with one of his steely eyed stares. "I believe I can do better," he said. Then he went to pick up his balls and hit them again.

The man just loved to practice. Mr. Hogan was famous for saying, "There is not enough daylight to practice all the shots." These are not the words of a man who thought of practice as a chore. He found joy in it. Practice was as much a part of his character as it was a means to an end. "People used to laugh at me because I practiced so much," he said. I think I reminded him why he loved to practice. Also, I am a visual learner and he quickly realized that he could get a lot more out of me by demonstrating than he could by speaking.

Words like *grinding* and *digging* were always used around him. He was a man who spent five hours hitting balls after making ten birdies and shooting 64. Most people would celebrate after that kind of round but Mr. Hogan always thought he could do better. He told me more than once about a reoccurring dream that he had. In it he played eighteen holes, hitting every green and every fairway and making every putt until he got to the 18th hole. He always woke up right before putting for his eighteenth birdie. "It makes me so damn mad." He would say, "I wish, just once, I would keep sleeping so I can make that birdie on 18!"

Once he slipped back into the familiar company of a shag bag and a flat spot of ground, he went full in. For days and weeks I would watch him hit every ball he had. When he tired, he would sit down and watch as I worked through my bag. Then we would go out together and pick up our balls. There was no rust on his compact, flat swing, a motion that has been studied by teachers and players for decades. Sequences of Mr. Hogan's golf swing rank among the most scrutinized and analyzed photographs since the Zapruder film. The clubhead speed wasn't quite what it was in the fifties, but the results were just as good as they had ever been. Mr. Hogan's shots had a distinct pop, a sound that was different from any other I'd heard. A ball never clanked off his clubface. Every swing resulted in a solid smack, with the ball cutting through the Texas sky like a rifle shot, and when he really liked a shot he would say, "That's got it."

One of the best lessons Mr. Hogan taught me was how to practice. It wasn't just about beating balls. It was about preparing to play golf. He would have me think about what shots were needed prior to each tournament and start practicing them before I got to the tournament. To him, every shot in practice had a purpose, and that purpose could be found somewhere on the golf course. He would only hit about twenty-five balls at a time. He felt if he hit any more than that he would lose focus. He loved having someone shag for him because it brought the target to life and gave him a little break while the balls were brought back. His goal was to keep the shag boy standing still and catch the ball on the first or second hop. The longer he could keep the shag boy in one spot, the more the pressure would increase, and the closer it became to a tournament situation. "It is like running the table in pool," he said. "The more you can create a golf course mentality on the practice tee, the easier it is to transition between practice and play." He always insisted that I finish my practice sessions with a short iron to get my tempo back. He was emphatic about never ending a practice session with a driver.

I'm surprised he still loved to practice so much because I know he was in a lot of pain. Sometimes he would wince when he swung, and sometimes I would see him catch himself when his knee would almost buckle. He would never talk about it, even if I asked, but it made sense that he had stopped practicing with any regularity. When his back finally felt loose enough for him to hit drivers, the shots rarely varied in distance, direction, or trajectory. His patterns with a driver were tighter than what I could get with my 9-iron. After hitting a couple of dozen drivers one afternoon, we went out to pick up the balls. All but one was in a ten-by-twenty-yard box.

"Where's my other ball?" he said.

One of the rules on the Little Nine was that you could only hit twenty-five balls at a time. He always knew exactly how many balls were in his shag bag and how many he had to pick up. We looked for a second, and then I spotted one twenty yards farther down.

"You're not going to believe this," I said as I picked it up.

When he saw it, he said, "Is it that damn Ultra?" He had gotten one hard Ultra ball mixed in his shag bag.

"It is," I said.

He shook his head and smiled. "I might have to play that ball."

Another time, as he was ripping one driver after another down the center, I said, "Wow, you're hitting it great today."

"It's this driver," he said. "You can't hit it off line. Give it a try."

By this time I had become very comfortable around him, but, still, hitting Ben Hogan's driver would make anyone nervous. The one thought screaming through my head was *Don't scrape a ball across the top and scuff this thing.* Then I swung the club and thought I'd torn a rotator cuff. I turned back to find him laughing. He just loved his little joke. To this day it remains the stiffest, heaviest club I've ever swung. When I attempted to hit a shot, the ball went dead right, just as Mr. Hogan knew it would. It turns out his driver was the heaviest ever measured by the USGA, and the joke was one he'd played on other people. He got a real kick out of convincing people to hit his driver. I think I hold the distinction of being the only woman to be on the receiving end of that prank.

I never asked him why he stopped practicing, but I assumed it was because of the pain. I've played in a lot of pain the last few years, so I can empathize with what he was fighting through. But I also know that he never stopped loving the grind, the learning, and the process of digging a swing out of the dirt.

Mr. Hogan practiced because it was in his nature, as much a part of his genetic code as his crystal blue eyes.

GETTING TO KNOW
THE REAL MR. HOGAN

❖

I know that above all, Mr. Hogan wanted to be remembered for being a gentleman. He loved golf and he loved winning tournaments but he wanted to be remembered for the person he was, not the golfer. I've met some amazing people in my life. When I meet people for the first time, I see their heart. I know that sounds a little strange. Most people notice eyes or a smile (or some other body part), but for me the first impression is always about the heart. I was pretty nervous when I was first getting to know Mr. Hogan, but when I got over that and was able to really see him for the person he was, I realized he was something special. I knew right away that he had a good heart. Sure, he was a bit crusty and abrupt at times, but I saw through that. Deep down he was a big softy with a very quick wit. I think people often missed his sense of humor because they were too nervous around him to see it.

I once asked him to sign a poster for Tommy Smothers.

"Put something funny on it," I said.

He thought about it for a minute and then wrote, "Tommy, give it up." Tommy loved it!

He was a stickler for presentation. He wore a jacket and tie to the office every day, even when the only person he would see was his secretary. There was never anything flashy about him, but everything was quality. I don't think I ever saw him without creased slacks and a pressed shirt, and he wore the most beautiful cashmere sweaters I'd ever seen. That, in his view, was the minimum presentation for a professional golfer. After winning the British Open, he finished playing, signed his card, and took the time to go into the locker room, comb his hair, and put on a sport coat. If you played the game for a living, Mr. Hogan thought you had an obligation to represent the game in your appearance. He hated all the "signs" worn by tour players on their hats and shirts. The business aspect of sponsorship didn't offend him—in fact he was one of the pioneers of the professional outing business, and all the players benefited from that—but turning professionals into billboards was something he thought cheapened the person and the game. I heard him grumble about it often.

Of course, Mr. Hogan had his quirks and eccentricities. He never took a bite of food without first polishing the silverware with a clean napkin or handkerchief, and he would scrub his hands, wrists, and forearms like a surgeon every time he came indoors. His arrival time at Shady Oaks rarely varied, and he walked through the clubhouse on the same route at the same pace, taking the same number of steps; he usually spoke to the same people in the same way, a "Hi" to the receptionist, an "Afternoon" to the bartender, and a "How are you today?" to his waitress. He would sit in the same chair at the same table in the grillroom where he ordered bean soup with a side order of bacon more often than not for lunch. He loved order, and he lived life like his pre-shot routine, consistent and uncomplicated. But from the stories I heard, he was also quite adventuresome. He loved to fly, having become a pilot during his time in the Army Air Corps. Most people know Arnold Palmer as a pilot-golfer, but few knew that Ben Hogan could barrel-roll a P-38 Lightning. He was also an expert horseman, as comfortable in the saddle as he was with a golf club in his hand.

"I didn't know you rode," I said to him after hearing about his horseback riding skills.

"My father was a blacksmith," he said. "I learned to ride before I learned to walk." Then he looked out the window as if lost in some melancholy memory.

A toe in the water was as deep as the conversations about his family usually got. He said his mother was a "strong woman," his sister "a good singer who enjoyed performing," and his brother, Royal, was "a very good baseball player, probably the best athlete in the family." But those comments only came as answers to my probing questions. He rarely volunteered. Royal Hogan was a member at Shady Oaks and he was always very kind to me. He owned Hogan's Office Supply store in downtown Fort Worth and had lunch at the club at least two or three times a week. They would speak to each other the way brothers do, but I never saw them pal around together, and Mr. Hogan never offered any deep insight into his relationship with his siblings.

In the beginning we talked about family only because I brought it up. I would always ask about Valerie and her sister, Sarah Harriman. He would respond with things like "They're doing fine." After I got to know him a little better, he would share nuggets about Valerie. She was the light of his life, and he never uttered an unkind word about her that I heard. I was much more open about my feelings and he could always tell if something was bothering me. During one of our Monday lunches I told him that Tom Byrum and I were breaking up partly because it was so difficult with both of us playing golf and him traveling all the time. Then I started to cry. I'm sure he didn't know what to do. He was patting my back and trying to say anything to make me feel better. He came up with "I'd have been delighted if Valerie had wanted to play golf." Then he declared Tom to be a "nothing divided by nothing," which he wasn't. Mr. Hogan liked Tom and did quite a bit to help him as he was working his way onto the tour. The comments were designed to support me, which was sweet and exactly what I wanted to hear at the time.

One night I had dinner at Shady Oaks with Mr. and Mrs. Hogan, and another boyfriend, Kirk Lucas, whom I would later marry. Mr. Hogan told a great story about some advice that Mrs. Hogan once gave him for his golf game. "I had come home from the course complaining that I hadn't made a single putt all day. I told her how frustrated I was and how I didn't know what to do about it." We were listening intently. "So she says to me, 'Well, Ben, why don't you just hit it closer?'" He laughed and we laughed along with him. "Hit it closer," he said. "So that's what I did."

They also told a great story about golf in their marriage. After a number of years of marriage, Mrs. Hogan decided that if she was going to spend this much time around golf she might as well try to play.

"I was thrilled she'd taken an interest in learning to play," Mr. Hogan said. "But she wouldn't go out on the course with me. So I said, 'Why don't you go out with Louise?'"

Louise was Louise Nelson, Byron Nelson's first wife. Mrs. Nelson and Mrs. Hogan were good friends, much closer, in fact, than Mr. Hogan and Mr. Nelson, even though the men had grown up together caddying at Glen Garden.

Then after some probing questions from Kirk, Mrs. Hogan told us. "Well, I took some lessons, although I don't know what that pro was trying to teach me," she said.

"I don't either," Mr. Hogan chimed in.

"Anyway," she continued with a wave of her hand, "I wasn't very good. So, finally, Louise and I were going out to play. The pro made a tee time for us. When we showed up there were at least fifty people standing around the first tee. Word had gotten out that Hogan and Nelson had a tee time. I don't know what everybody thought, but I'm sure they didn't come out to watch us."

That got a hearty laugh from everyone at the table.

"Tell them about the caddy," Mr. Hogan said.

"Oh, yes," she said. "We played a round. Again, neither of us was any good, but we were having a grand time. And then we got on one of the last holes and I had a shot from the rough, and I said to my caddy, 'What club should I hit?' He just shook his head, and said, 'Mrs. Hogan, it really doesn't matter.'" Mr. Hogan loved that line.

Kirk's nature is to ask a lot of questions, and this night was no exception. Kirk understood the historic significance of having dinner with the Hogans. He wasn't going to let the opportunity pass him by without getting as many questions answered as possible. At one point Mr. Hogan leaned toward me and asked, "Is this fella a reporter?" Mrs. Hogan hit him in the shoulder and said, "Now, Ben, you know he isn't." We all laughed and Kirk kept right on asking questions. I'm sure his instincts would have been shared by most people. Every serious golfer had at least one question they wanted to ask Mr. Hogan.

I was never like that, which might have been why Mr. Hogan and I got along so well. We talked more about life and friends and what we'd had for dinner the night before than we did about golf. It was nothing earth-shattering, just two friends chatting about whatever came to mind. He would tell stories about his early caddying days at Glen Garden, a seven-mile walk from his house, but a trek he didn't mind at all. It was good money and it gave him a chance to be around the game that he grew to love. I would later learn more Spartan tales from that time, like the one about him selling papers on the train platform, but always saving two papers. Later, after carrying golf bags for thirty-six holes, he would spread one paper out in a bunker to sleep on, and use the other as a blanket so that he could be the first caddy at the course the following morning.

For decades people have speculated about his relationship with Valerie, and how their personalities meshed. I saw them as a classic American romance. Even after fifty years of marriage, he always opened doors for her, held her chair when they sat down to eat, and stood whenever she left the table. He would get tears in his eyes as he recounted the many sacrifices she made for him.

I remember calling him from Atlanta after the second round of the U.S. Open. That was not unusual. I talked to him after many of my tournament rounds. As I was recounting how I'd played, he said, "Would you stop lollygagging! What are you doing out there? I want you to go out there and start by thinking about the green, where you want to be and how you want to get there, and then work your way back, practicing until you can make every shot."

He was right, of course, and I was accustomed to his blunt assessments, especially when I screwed up. I hung up the phone laughing and went out to practice. When I got back to Shady Oaks two days later, I was at the bar talking to Sandy, the bartender, when Mr. Hogan walked in and asked if he had insulted me the other day. I was thinking, *You insult me at least once a day. What "other day" are you talking about?* All I could say, though, was "Huh?"

"Valerie says I insulted you the other day when you called me from the Open," he said. "She said I was curt and rude. She hasn't talked to me all weekend."

I bit my lip to keep from laughing, but it didn't work. I could almost hear her getting onto him, and I cracked up. He did too. He had that sparkle in his eye that I loved, so after I gathered myself, I said, "Do you need me to call her?"

"Would you mind?" he replied.

I dialed the number and Valerie answered on the second ring.

"Mrs. Hogan," I said, "I just wanted you to know that Mr. Hogan didn't insult me the other day. If he didn't talk to me like that, I'd think he didn't love me anymore."

"Oh, Kris," she said, "I know you know how he is, but I was so worried about you." So worried was she, in fact, that she had called the pro shop at the Atlanta Athletic Club and tried to find me. She had visions of me crying in a corner somewhere. That was even funnier. I had gotten a lot harsher tongue lashings from my ballet teacher, Carolyn, when I was growing up. That was another reason Mr. Hogan and I got along so well, I knew he was gruff with me because he cared. When he stopped saying anything was when I would start worrying.

It was amazing we were so close because we were so different. Other than the story about Valerie and Louise Nelson playing golf, he never told a golf story involving his family. At times I had trouble telling one that didn't involve mine. Golf was inseparable from any discussion of the Tschetters. We belonged to Minnehaha Country Club. The name is from the Dakota language, meaning "waterfall," but is best known as the name of Hiawatha's wife in Longfellow's poem. Mom had a decent game but we always teased her that we could add up everyone else's handicap in the family, multiply it by three, and it still wouldn't add up to the shots she needed. Dad and my brother Mike were both scratch. I had a two handicap growing up, and my brother Eric, who is five years younger than I, was about a five. Mom carried a twenty-three handicap, which was very respectable in the ladies golf association, but earned her immeasurable grief at home.

We played every day the weather permitted. We probably wouldn't have spent as much time with Dad if we hadn't played golf. As young kids we all had our scheduled days to caddy for him. Mike was on Wednesday afternoon (men's day). My day was Saturday, and Eric worked Dad's bag on Sunday. I got paid $4.50 and gave him a free round for his birthday and Father's Day.

Mom would always let us out of our chores if we were going to the golf course, and conversations at the dinner table centered around who shot what that day. One of the standard sayings in our family was "Start on 17," which meant we didn't need to hear about every shot on every hole, just the last two. Mike once played seventy-two holes in one day, carrying his bag the whole way. He got to "start on 17" four times that night.

I got the sense that Mr. Hogan loved hearing stories about my family as much as I loved telling them. He knew both of my brothers. Eric started at TCU in 1988, and it didn't take long for him to give Eric the nickname Ass-n-Elbows. Mr. Hogan didn't spend the time with either of my brothers that he did with me, but he was exceptionally generous with all of us, giving tips to Mike and Eric, and always keeping up with how they were playing. But he would also rib us. One day as we were hitting balls, he asked if "Ass-n-Elbows" was going to join us. Eric has a great sense of humor and is even more of a talker than I am. He added even more lightheartedness to our practice sessions when he showed up. Mr. Hogan called it "the sideshow" when he was there, because the banter would go up a level. So when Eric got there that day, Mr. Hogan joined in with the joking, teasing, and laughing. Eric finally asked him, "Mr. Hogan, why do you call me Ass-n-Elbows?"

"Because of how you flail those bony arms and that butt of yours when you're trying to hit a golf ball," he said, and then he would give an exaggerated demonstration of Eric's pre-shot routine, which did involve a lot of fidgeting. "You look like a barnyard chicken."

We all got a kick out of that. What the rest of us didn't know at the time was that Mr. Hogan also gave Eric some serious advice. "You could be the best player in the family," he said. "You've just got to practice more. You love to play, but playing isn't learning. You need to practice every shot you could have on the course before going out there. It seems to me you want to try to wing it on the course. You're pretty good, but if you want to get better, you need to put in the time."

It was a simple theme, but one Mr. Hogan believed in above all others. For decades, devotees of the game have searched for Hogan's "secret," as if it were some lost artifact or hidden treasure. He wrote about it in *Life* magazine in the fifties, claiming that he rotated his forearm to get the clubface open, thus eliminating the hook. That sparked a virtual revolution in instruction, with teachers suddenly focusing on pronating the forearms on the backswing and supinating them on the downswing. But in all my time with him, Mr. Hogan never once said the word *pronation*, nor did we ever discuss the radial flexor or the carpi ulnaris muscles of the forearm.

He paid a lot of attention to plane, insisting many times that in order to groove a repeating swing the club had to travel on a plane that was below a line from the golf ball through the top of your shoulders. That was his famous "pane of glass." By keeping your arm and the club beneath the imaginary pane of glass you could groove a consistent, repetitive golf swing. He never talked about rotating the forearms in the backswing, but he would grab my wrists with his big hand and rotate them on the follow-through, saying that you could hit the ball as hard as you wanted to without fearing that it would go left as long as you had a good grip. From what he told me, if you put your hands on the club properly, the face would naturally rotate open on the backswing and back to square on the way down. Grip and setup were the keys to getting the clubface in the right position.

I've often thought that the "left hand is the steering wheel and right hand is the gas" article he kept threatening to write was how the whole "secret" thing got started. He probably told a *Life* magazine writer that he was going to write another article and that snowballed into "Hogan's Secret!" I can almost see Mr. Hogan laughing that such a big deal was being made about a little article he was going to write. When asked, he always said the secret was in the dirt. Maybe his secret, if there was one, was simply daily practice. He told me that if he took a day off it would take him a week to work back to where he was. He thought that the key to great golf was work, a relentless pursuit of perfection, repeating the swing through hours and hours of practice. Another great performer, jazz musician Branford Marsalis, once told me, "There is no such thing as downtime. If you've got a few extra minutes, you can always practice." I think Branford and his brother Wynton learned that lesson from their father, and I'm sure Mr. Hogan would have agreed. No matter where you were or what you were doing, he believed you should either be practicing or thinking about practice.

Mrs. Hogan enjoyed telling a story about staying in a cheap motel early in their married life. At two A.M. the manager called because Mr. Hogan was practicing his chipping into a metal chair and the walls were so thin that he was keeping the people in the adjacent rooms awake. "When I was asked how I felt about my husband practicing his chipping in the middle of the night, I said that since we were relying on his golf for our living, I didn't mind it at all."

Mr. Hogan preached practice throughout his life, sometimes going so far that people thought he was being rude. If someone who never went to the range approached him with a question about the golf swing, his typical response was something like "It doesn't matter if you don't practice."

He never said that to me, I guess because I hit so many balls. He also appreciated the work ethic my brother Mike showed. I hit a lot of balls but Mike hit twice as many as I did. He didn't teach Mike, but he was always watching. One afternoon early in our tenure as members at Shady Oaks, Mr. Hogan went over to where Mike was hitting balls and watched him for several minutes without a word. Then he looked at Mike's clubs. They were Hogan irons and woods, the right brand, but Mike had hit so many balls that the faces were worn smooth. When Mike finished practicing Mr. Hogan said, "Come by my office tomorrow. We need to get you in some new clubs."

It was almost as though he adopted the Tschetter children while they were in Fort Worth. Even though he spent the least amount of time on the lesson tee with Mike, he never neglected him. After Mike graduated and turned pro he stayed in Fort Worth and is still in the area twenty-five years later.

One day Mr. Hogan approached him and said, "Would you like to play in the Colonial?" He was talking about the Colonial National Invitational, the PGA Tour event.

"I'd love to," Mike said, "but I don't have my tour card yet. I don't think I'll get invited."

"Let me see what I can do," Mr. Hogan said.

So, when two members of the tournament committee came to ask Mr. Hogan if he would be attending the Champions Dinner, Mr. Hogan asked if it would be possible to give Mike an invitation to the tournament. Sponsor's exemptions are more precious than gold on tour. Scores of players, many of them well-known players, are vying for them, writing letters, making phone calls and, in effect, begging. The tournament director is given two to four sponsor's exemptions, which are, in essence, gifts. They are invitations to join the field because of some marketing value, or loyalty, or simply because the director thinks they add value to his event.

Years later, Colonial became the center of the golf universe when they gave Annika Sörenstam a sponsor's exemption, making her the first woman in fifty years to compete in a PGA Tour event. Mike didn't expect to get into the Colonial, even after Mr. Hogan offered. It was a nice gesture, but somebody at the tour would certainly quash the idea.

The men from the tournament committee told Mr. Hogan that sponsor's exemptions were rare commodities, so Mr. Hogan said, "Well, just give him my invitation." The committee continued to invite Mr. Hogan to play in the Colonial, even though he hadn't played a tournament round in two decades.

They weren't sure what to say. They didn't give him an answer right away, so Mr. Hogan didn't answer their question either. When they called on him again to see if he had considered coming to the dinner he asked if they had considered Mike Tschetter's invitation. The tournament director paused for a long moment before saying, "We're still considering it." Then he said, "We look forward to seeing you at the Champions Dinner this year, Mr. Hogan."

Mr. Hogan came back with "I'll certainly consider it."

At that time he didn't attend every Champions Dinner,

but the possibility of his attending was one of the main reasons the event was so successful. No past champion would turn down an opportunity to have dinner with Mr. Hogan. By all accounts he was very animated at these dinners, regaling the attendees with stories and playing the perfect host, surprising many with his affability.

Not a lot of people realize that Mr. Hogan was the person behind the Champions Dinner at the Masters. Years before, he had approached Bobby Jones and said, "We should have all the champions get together. Send me the bill." Since then, the reigning champion has picked out the menu and picked up the tab for the Masters Champions Dinner. And while he didn't initiate the dinner at Colonial, Mr. Hogan was instrumental in its growth. To have him beat around the bush about coming had to send a jolt through the tournament committee.

A few days later Mike got an invitation to play in the Colonial National Invitational and Mr. Hogan attended the Champions Dinner.

Mr. Hogan was never very forthcoming about his life experiences, like many from his generation who had lived through the Great Depression and World War II. Sharing details about their lives and families was either boasting or airing dirty laundry. I couldn't even get him to talk about saving Valerie's life in that horrific 1949 car crash. Almost forgotten in this story is that Mr. Hogan's first instinct was to protect his wife by throwing his body in front of her to save her from serious injury. Yet, when I asked him about saving Valerie, he couldn't change the subject fast enough. "Happened so fast, nobody really had time to think" was all he would say. I also asked him if he ever hit the ball as well after his accident. "Not even close," he said. End of story.

He kept the extent of his injuries a secret. Everyone knew that Mr. Hogan's legs had been badly damaged and that a blood clot that formed while he was in the hospital almost killed him. All those facts were well publicized at the time, as was the fact that he had to wear bandages and stockings when he was competing, and braces on his legs later in life. What he didn't tell a lot of people was that the crash damaged his left eye, and his sight got worse and worse with each passing year. By the time I got to know him, he was almost completely blind in his left eye, which caused problems with his depth perception. To understand how big a problem it was, try hitting a golf ball with your left eye closed. Unless you have extraordinary muscle memory, you're going to struggle with your ball striking and it makes the feel shots around the green particularly difficult. Mr. Hogan did, occasionally, hit a bad shot but I think it had more to do with him losing sight of the ball in his back swing. I don't think anyone watching him hit a golf ball would ever know that he wasn't perfectly healthy and at least a decade younger than his age.

As great as he struck it, I asked him if he ever considered going to Augusta and hitting the ceremonial first shot—a great theatrical moment that Gene Sarazen, Sam Snead, and Byron Nelson shared at the time. When Gene passed away and Byron got too feeble to swing, Snead went at it alone for a couple of years. After he passed away Arnold Palmer assumed the mantle, now joined by Jack Nicklaus. I always got the sense that Mr. Hogan would have enjoyed it, but he said that after a lifetime on the road he was tired of traveling. Still, if it hadn't been for the eye causing him to mishit a shot every now and then, I think he would have been on the first tee at Augusta on Thursday morning. I wish he had gone, because I'm telling you, he rarely ever hit a bad shot!

Even though he regularly shared his expertise with me, I recognized a reluctance when it came to helping others. I think he was afraid of making people's swings worse and he was only willing to help someone if he thought they would be willing to work at it. He knew that I wanted to learn and would put in the time.

We were hitting balls on the little nine one day when a group of men came to the 18th tee ready to tee off. We were close enough to bother them if we didn't halt our practice session so we waited while they teed off. Afterward there was an awkward silence that, of course, I had to fill. I went on and on about what a slave driver he was and how it was impossible to do the things with a golf ball he wanted me to do. They all laughed and he stood there with his arms crossed, waiting for me to finish so we could get back at it. Any time our practice was interrupted, I could see the annoyance on his face. (Eric was the exception. He loved it when Ass-n-Elbows showed up.)

I didn't take friends out with me to practice because I knew that doing so would probably keep him from joining me, or at least make him hesitant about hitting any balls. By this time he understood that every action he took would end up being a story. *I saw Ben Hogan hit a ball today*, or *Ben Hogan said good morning to me as I was changing shoes in the locker room*. Those stories, no matter how innocuous, would outlive him, and he didn't want anybody saying anything after he was gone like *I saw Ben Hogan hit practice balls once and he didn't hit it as pure as I expected*. Everything resulted in a story and you wouldn't believe how long a person can drag out a "Hogan" story. My husband is no exception. One of his favorite stories is about the first time he saw him hit a golf shot. Having dined with the Hogans the night before, Mr. Hogan knew Kirk and didn't mind having him join us for our practice session. We were practicing in a strong right-to-left wind and Mr. Hogan was trying to get me to move the ball back into it. He wasn't hitting at all by then, but I knew if I didn't achieve what he was asking of me he might hit a few shots, and I really wanted Kirk to have the once-in-a-lifetime chance to see him swing. I was hitting it pretty straight with a few big hooks thrown in for good measure.

"Make it move left to right!" I'm sure he was thinking, *You klutz!* but he was too much of a gentleman to say it.

"It must be turning a little bit," I said. "That is a strong wind!"

"No, it's not. Make it curve!" He could get very frustrated with me at times but it never bothered me.

I handed him my club. "Show me."

He grabbed my 6-iron and without warming up or taking a single practice swing he hit a perfect iron shot that fought its way through the wind curving from left to right.

"I missed it. Could you hit one more?" I said. He was onto me but he hit another exactly like the first. Then he hit one more just to prove his point and handed the club back to me, telling me it was my turn.

Kirk said it was like going back in time. It was exactly like every piece of film he had ever seen of him. No one put their hands on the club like Mr. Hogan and age hadn't changed that or the swing one bit. Watching him hit a shot was everything he had hoped for. The grip, the setup, the waggle, the swing, and the flight of the ball were perfect. But the most memorable thing was the sound. It was unforgettable, truly unique.

He was stunned that a man that age required no stretching or warming up. There was no thought to it. Mr. Hogan just stepped into the shot and went back in time. (It takes Kirk at least five minutes to tell this story.)

I'm glad Kirk got the chance to watch Mr. Hogan hit those shots. It really was something to see. He probably would have hit one if I had just asked. He never said no when I asked him for something for my family. He was always polite to my father whenever they spoke. When I got my first invitation to the Dinah Shore, Dad called Mr. Hogan to let him know that I had made it into the field. Without my knowing, Mr. Hogan had tried to get me into the tournament by calling Dinah Shore, but the rules were the rules and at the time you had to have finished first, second, or third in an event to get in. At Tucson I birdied the last six holes on Sunday, to finish second, which got me into the season's first major. After some polite chitchat, Dad said, "Mr. Hogan, I just want to thank you for the interest you've taken in my children and for all the things you've done for them."

"No," Mr. Hogan said, "it is I who thank you for allowing me to get to know your family. It's been very special for me."

That was the kind of man he was. As we became closer and I got more comfortable sharing things with him, I would periodically tell him I wanted to introduce him to someone the next day. "Mr. Hogan, I've got somebody I'd like you to meet tomorrow," I'd say.

"I've already met all the people I want to meet," he'd reply with a faux gruffness in his voice.

"Yes, but that's what you said before you met me."

The opening bars of a smile would slip softly onto his face. He'd get that sparkle in his eye and say, "Worst day of my life."

Mr. Hogan was naturally shy and with his fame came a cautiousness, so meeting new people made him a bit uneasy. I think he felt that most people either wanted something from him or only cared about meeting Ben Hogan the golfer. He enjoyed meeting new people because he knew he could probably learn something from them, but he wanted to be Ben Hogan, the man, not the golfer when they were talking. What he didn't enjoy was meeting someone if he couldn't devote himself fully to them. It was better, in his view, not to meet someone if it meant giving that person only half of his attention, or worse, no attention at all. It's a different approach from the one many of today's celebrities take. My pal Charles Barkley, for instance, believes that if he gives someone a minute, or even thirty seconds, it could make their day or even their year. He handles being a celebrity better than anyone I know because Charles doesn't let it stop him from getting out and living his life. When you meet him you feel like you are the most important person in the world for that minute he's with you. Mr. Hogan felt that the people he met were owed more than that. And if he couldn't give them some time, he would rather not meet them at all.

I always assumed that was one of the reasons for the unwritten rule at Shady Oaks about not speaking to Mr. Hogan. If all the people who wanted to meet him walked up and introduced themselves, the man would never have a second to himself. In his view, making a new acquaintance required not only speaking, but listening and learning, two things Mr. Hogan did very well, but things that required time. If he was going to spend time with you, he thought you deserved his best. Anything less would be an insult to the person he was meeting, and he wouldn't stand for that.

On the social front, he and I were polar opposites. The more people I met, the better. Part of the thrill of going to a new place was meeting people, or so I thought. Being young, I never fully understood or appreciated Mr. Hogan's apprehension when it came to new acquaintances. What he knew that I didn't at the time was that every person he met would walk away with a story, an impression of Ben Hogan that they would share with dozens, perhaps hundreds, of their friends. He understood that if he didn't say the right things, or if the person he met took something the wrong way, the repercussions would have a ripple effect.

Mr. Hogan humored me when I brought new people by to meet him, especially boyfriends. He was like my grandfather, and he enjoyed being able to critique them. When I would ask him what he thought, he would let me know straightaway if they were, in his words, "no good," or worse, "a nothing divided by nothing." The mildest criticism he would offer was "He wears his hair a little long for my liking." If that was all he said, I figured I had a keeper.

It was during one of those boyfriend conversations that Mr. Hogan shared one of his most guarded secrets with me, a devastating bit of history that explained a lot of things while churning up many more unanswered questions. It was one of those out-of-the-blue moments that caught me by surprise, but it has stayed with me forever. He had already proclaimed one of the guys I'd taken to meet him as being "no good," following it up with "You can do a lot better."

Being young, I tried to defend my friend. "I know, Mr. Hogan, but you have to understand, his parents are divorced, and he had a pretty hard childhood. It's been a tough time for him."

"Tough time?" he said quietly. "I'll tell you about a tough time. Imagine a little boy walking into a room as . . ." His voice trailed off, but he stuck out his index finger like a gun and made the unmistakable gesture of a man shooting himself. He looked at me as if surprised by what he had just said. Tears welled up in his eyes. He had this hollow, shattered look on his face, one I had never seen from him before and one that I will never forget. His eyes fell to the floor and then into the distance. It was as if he thought that focusing on something far off would push the words and memories away.

I had no idea that Mr. Hogan's father had killed himself.

Nobody outside his immediate family did, and even some of them were in the dark. Valerie didn't know until she was told by Mr. Hogan's sister, and that was after they had been together for several years. The suicide of a parent isn't something you bring up in casual conversation, so the fact that he didn't share it with many people was not unusual, but I don't think anybody outside Valerie and his siblings knew that Mr. Hogan, at age nine, had been in the room when his father, Chester, took his own life with a .38 caliber revolver.

I was stunned for a moment. Then I said, "Mr. Hogan, what do you mean?"

He didn't look at me as he shook his head, waving his hands. "Never mind," he said.

I didn't know what to say, so I gave him a hug. "Never mind," he said again.

I think it stunned him as much as me that he had told me that. He never mentioned it to me again, and I never brought it up. For a brief moment, I caught a glimpse of another Hogan Secret, the life-altering experience on which every aspect of the man was built: his drive, his introversion, his caution in developing meaningful human contacts.

I have never told anyone other than my family about our conversation until now. The facts of Chester Hogan's suicide have been picked clean by journalists and media-happy psychologists eager to analyze a man they never met. But his friends, for the most part, remained silent on the subject. I've decided to share it, because this incident showed that Mr. Hogan didn't run away from the most traumatic experience imaginable, and he wasn't in denial. His father's suicide affected him, and he knew it. It still brought tears to his eyes sixty-five years later.

I continued taking people out to meet him, and I still let him pass judgment on my boyfriends. He even gave an approving nod to Kirk, although Kirk wore his hair a little longer than Mr. Hogan liked. But I never again told him that anyone had gone through "a tough time." Such a statement required perspective. And Mr. Hogan had a lot more of that than I could ever comprehend.

"I TRIED TO QUIT THE GAME
THOUSANDS OF TIMES."

Of all the times I introduced people to Mr. Hogan, the most enlightening meeting came when I took Dr. Bob Rotella, one of the world's most famous sports psychologists, out to Shady Oaks. "Doc," as all his clients call Rotella, pioneered the concept of sports psychology as a coachable practice, and on any given week, he could be found at tour events standing beside all the swing and short-game coaches. He has worked as a consultant for the PGA Tour, the LPGA Tour, the NFL, NBA, Major League Baseball, NASCAR, and the U.S. Olympic Ski Team, and his book *Golf Is Not a Game of Perfect* is the third best-selling golf book of all time. The number one best-selling golf book is Ben Hogan's *Five Lessons: The Modern Fundamentals of Golf*, an instructional masterpiece that barely touches on the mental aspect of the game. That was why I thought this meeting would be interesting. Doc said things like "Golf is about how well you accept, respond to, and score with your misses much more so than it is a game of your perfect shots." Mr. Hogan once hit balls for hours after shooting a course-record 64 because he felt he had mishit too many shots.

I had no idea how the two of them would get along or what they would talk about, but I felt like the conversation would be worth hearing. I'd worked with Doc on my focus and mental preparation for some time, so I asked him if he'd like to meet the man who had helped me with my swing.

Doc was thrilled, but I wasn't sure how Mr. Hogan would feel. Men of his generation thought psychology was for psychos. Jackie Burke, another Texan and contemporary of Mr. Hogan's who won the 1956 Masters and PGA Championship, once said, "Back when we played, everybody had the same sports psychologist. His name was Jack Daniel." I had never heard Mr. Hogan offer an opinion on sports psychology, so when I brought up the idea one afternoon as we were practicing I was pleasantly surprised when he didn't give me his usual grumble or patented "I've met all the people I need to meet" response. He looked directly at me a few seconds without saying anything—the kind of uncomfortable pause that turned those who didn't know him into nervous bowls of jelly—and then he nodded slowly and said, "That's fine. Let me know when he'd like to come out."

At the time, Doc was working with several players who lived in the area, including Tom Kite and David Frost. I said, "The next time you're in Dallas, I'll set it up. You can drive over, meet Mr. Hogan, and we'll play Shady Oaks."

Several weeks later, Doc was in town working with Frost and staying at his house in Dallas. I asked Mr. Hogan if he had a few minutes to spare, and he said he was looking forward to the meeting.

Doc had grown up playing a lot of different sports, with golf well down on the list. While he was excited about spending some time with Mr. Hogan, he was not as enthralled by the Hogan Mystique as someone who'd been a Hogan fan since youth. But he was still nervous. Like a lot of people, Doc had heard stories about Mr. Hogan's testy and less than conversational persona. The night before he was to drive out to Shady Oaks, Doc sat in Frost's study running through all the things he wanted to ask Mr. Hogan, and anticipating how things might go. Looking through Frost's bookshelf for something that might stimulate conversation, he found a copy of the 1954 classic *Bobby Locke on Golf.* Locke, a South African Hall of Famer who won four British Opens, had married a woman from Doc's hometown of Rutland, Vermont. When he pulled out the book and thumbed through it, Doc immediately found his conversation starter for the meeting with Mr. Hogan.

The next afternoon I met Doc at the club and took him to the grillroom, where Mr. Hogan was waiting at his table. The two men shook hands like old friends, and after a few introductory pleasantries, Doc started by saying, "Mr. Hogan, we have something in common. I was a caddy as a kid at my home club in Vermont."

"There's no better way to be introduced to the game," Mr. Hogan said.

"Well, while I was there I had the opportunity to caddy for Bobby Locke. His wife was from Rutland, and they summered there."

Mr. Hogan's eyebrows went up. He leaned a little closer, genuinely interested in where this story was going.

"So, last night as I was looking through David Frost's bookshelf, I found Locke's book," Doc said. "In one chapter, he designed his 'ideal' golfer, picking a player that he deemed 'perfect' for each particular club or shot. Did you realize that the only club he picked you for was the putter?"

Mr. Hogan smiled, remembering that.

"That surprised me. I'd heard that you were perhaps the best ball-striker of all time, but that you weren't a great putter."

Mr. Hogan's response was: "I was a great putter when I was winning tournaments. When I couldn't putt anymore, I quit."

Left unsaid was the fact that Mr. Hogan's deteriorating eyesight had as much to do with his poor putting as the "yips" or any of the other nerve-jangling maladies that have long been discussed in 19th holes around the world. Many suggested that he putted badly because he was naturally left-handed but played right-handed, so he had trouble developing putting touch. Not only did that not make any physiological sense, it was wrong on the facts. He was right-handed. I'd also heard that he didn't think putting was an important part of the game, so he didn't practice it. That's not true, he practiced his putting as much as anyone, and during his playing days he practiced putting more than most. Once the sun went down, he would roll putts in his hotel throughout the night.

"For a long time I hit the ball awful," he said. "Given how bad I hit it, I had to be a good putter to finish a round. Once I worked out the problems in my golf swing and got to hitting the ball fairly well, I was happy that I had missed so many fairways and greens early on, because it forced me to learn to be a good putter."

I had never heard Mr. Hogan speak of his putting like that, but it made sense. Nobody won sixty-four PGA Tour events and nine major championships without being a great putter.

"You take the U.S. Open at Merion, for instance," Mr. Hogan said. This was the famous comeback when he won the Open sixteen months after almost being killed in his car crash and being told he would probably never play golf again. "Everybody sees that picture of me hitting 1-iron on the last hole, and they love that pose and all, but today people assume I hit that shot to a foot and tapped in for birdie to win. The truth is I hit it forty feet left of the hole and made one of the greatest two-putts of my life to get into a play-off the next day. Folks today don't want to hear the truth. They don't want to know that I hit it left of the hole and had to hit two real good putts just to tie the lead and play eighteen more holes the next day. They'd rather think I hit it to a foot to win."

He talked quite a bit about Valerie, leaning in and gesturing with his hands to emphasize what was, to him, an important point. Since he was speaking with a sports psychologist, he thought he should tell some stories about his state of mind during this playing career. Mr. Hogan said to Doc, "Given what you do and the tour players you work with, something I think you can share with them, something that nobody knows, is that I tried to quit this game thousands of times, because I didn't feel like I was taking care of my wife in the manner I should have. I was living week to week. If we had forty dollars to our names, that was big. We were staying in crummy hotels and driving broken-down cars. That was no way to live and certainly no way to take care of a wife.

"I felt terrible, always skimping on things, having to find the cheapest restaurants and buy the cheapest things. It was not bad for me, because I had grown up poor and could survive no matter what, but I felt terrible for Valerie. Here she was married to a fellow that I'm sure she thought was going to provide a good life for her, and instead my golf game was just terrible. I tried to quit over and over, thousands of times, but Valerie wouldn't let me. She kept saying, 'You can't give up now. You're so close. I just know it.' This was a woman who didn't know the first thing about golf, but she knew her husband. I think she knew that I'd never be happy if I quit before I won championships. So, in a lot of ways, in those days, my wife was my sports psychologist.

"This is something I think you need to tell the players you work with. This image of me being a rock with no emotions is untrue. This game beat the devil out of me and brought me to my knees many, many times. Many nights I'd wake up in the hotel room at three or four in the morning wondering what on earth I was doing. I'd jump out of bed and hit putts or chips until the front desk called because somebody had complained about the racket. I'd wake up Valerie every time, but she never said anything. I guess when you've got forty dollars and you need a hundred to get home, you don't tell your husband to stop practicing, even in the middle of the night."

His internal drive came from many sources, his poverty-stricken upbringing, his father's suicide, the toughness it took to literally fight older, bigger caddies for a job. But here he was crediting Valerie for his inner drive. I didn't doubt for a minute that he believed it, but I also knew that he was tough, and he enjoyed defying the odds and doing what others thought couldn't be done.

Because of my loose joints, I started having shoulder

problems when I was seventeen. My shoulder was so loose that sometimes it would partially pop out of the socket (subluxation) when I swung. My parents took me to several doctors and we got several different opinions. It wasn't until the end of my first year on tour that it got serious. It was popping out more often than not and a series of doctors told me that I would never play professional golf with this condition. One specialist in Los Angeles was recommending total reconstructive surgery on both shoulders, a procedure that would sideline me for at least a year, probably longer, and offered no guarantee of success. Even the most optimistic doctors said I would always be limited in how much I could practice and how long I could play.

I remember talking to Mr. Hogan about it. I was upset and Mr. Hogan knew it. When he asked me what was wrong, I told him, "Every doctor I talk to is telling me that with my shoulders I'll never be able to play professional golf. Some are telling me to get surgery, others are telling me never to get surgery. I don't know what to do."

He nodded and gave me a sad, knowing smile. He took my hand and put it on his shoulder and said, "Feel this shoulder." It felt like his shoulder was hanging about two inches below where it should have been, almost like he had no shoulder at all. "My shoulder hurt so bad after the car accident that they finally took a good part of it out. Now it doesn't hurt." Left unsaid was the fact that most humans couldn't play golf without the sections of his shoulder that were now missing.

"Don't believe the doctors," he said. "They told me I'd never walk again, but I knew they were wrong. If you want it bad enough, you can do it. You can do anything you set your mind to."

Mr. Hogan's struggles were an inspiration for me. There were plenty of times when I was in the doctor's office or sitting in the locker room with ice on my shoulder that I could have said, "That's it. It's not worth it." But I had seen what Mr. Hogan had overcome, and I remembered his message. I could, indeed, do anything I set my mind to. I was also fortunate that a friend recommended that I see Keith Kleven, an amazing physical therapist in Las Vegas. He gave me a unique shoulder exercise regime and I was able to avoid the surgery. He has helped me with many different physical problems throughout the years. I have no doubt that he saved my career and I will always be grateful to him.

That memory came to mind as I listened to him talk to Doc Rotella. Mr. Hogan would never have liked being called a sports psychologist, but he always seemed to have the right words for me when I needed them most. To Doc, he tried to clear up some of the misconceptions about himself. "Valerie and I very frequently went out to dinner with other players and their wives, but I didn't talk much on the golf course," he said.

"Why?" Doc asked.

"Well, I was always afraid somebody would start a conversation about something that would interest me and it would distract me from what I was trying to do," he said. "I was so broke I couldn't afford to talk to other people, because I was afraid of losing my focus. So I stayed to myself on the golf course, and that again became one of the things that got blown out of proportion with time."

Doc then asked him about the famous Claude Harmon story. Claude, the 1948 Masters winner, was one of Mr. Hogan's best friends on tour. They played most of their major championship practice rounds together and had a lot of games at Seminole, the private club in Palm Beach where the two men and their families spent their winters. In the 1947 Masters, Claude and Mr. Hogan were paired together. According to legend, when they got to the famous par-3 12th, Mr. Hogan hit first and the ball stopped four feet below the hole. Then Claude hit a 7-iron and made a hole in one. The crowd went wild. Claude waved to the cheering gallery as he crossed the bridge over Rae's Creek. Then he waved again as he took the ball out of the hole. Mr. Hogan then rolled his birdie putt in the hole. According to the story that Claude told thousands of times, and that his sons, Butch, Craig, and Billy, have continued to spread, Mr. Hogan said, "Claude, I think that's the first time I've ever birdied that hole. What did you make?"

"Is it true?" Doc asked Mr. Hogan.

Mr. Hogan smiled. "I knew he'd made a one. I always felt

it was my obligation as a golfer to watch my playing partner's ball," he said. "I never watched them swing, but I watched the ball. He knew I was just teasing him, but it did make a great story."

Then he said, tongue in cheek, "That's the sort of thing that legends are made of."

To my eternal shock, Mr. Hogan revealed to Doc that his father had committed suicide when he was very young. He went on to say that he'd read a lot of books on families of suicide, and that it wasn't unusual for children of a suicidal parent to become loners.

Mr. Hogan was an avid reader and learner all his life. Then he mentioned his alter ego, Henny Bogan, and I knew the serious conversation was over. He brought him out when he wanted to lighten the mood. When someone asked him if he'd done something funny or nice he would say, "No, that was Henny Bogan." It was his way of deflecting praise, as if he were saying Ben Hogan wouldn't have done or said that. It must have been Henny Bogan.

Then the conversation moved on to the golf swing and Mr. Hogan shared the familiar story about finding the key to his swing in weakening his left-hand grip. As with all swing improvements a chain reaction occurred. He went into great detail about how his new grip allowed him to get the butt of the club pointed at his belt buckle and his triceps close to his sides. It also got the clubface more open in his backswing and allowed him to hit it with his right hand and hit it hard without worrying about "that damn hook." It always amazed me how meticulously Mr. Hogan analyzed the grip and setup. Whether it was the position of the feet relative to the line of play at address or making sure the left hip was a little higher than his right at address, Mr. Hogan believed there were no unimportant aspects to the setup. On that front, Doc and Mr. Hogan were in total agreement.

Then Mr. Hogan said, "A lot of my practice, especially in the military, was shadow swinging."

"What do you mean?" Doc asked.

Mr. Hogan said, "I mean there weren't video cameras back then. We had movie cameras, but they weighed two hundred pounds and had to be rolled on trailer beds. If you wanted to see your swing you had to either look in a mirror or find a place where the shadows were cast just right and watch your shadow." Doc was familiar with that because his father had been a battalion boxing champion in the navy.

Mr. Hogan nodded. "I would get up before revelry and use the moonlight to see my shadow. I'd swing a couple of hundred times, watching and feeling my swing. Most of my practice during that time was through feeling my golf swing in the dark. That was how you learned back then, through feel and watching the golf ball."

"What do you say to people who claim that, especially in your book, you didn't do what you said you did in your golf swing?" Doc asked.

Mr. Hogan's answer was great. He said, "I described what I felt. That's all I could do. I don't know if I was doing it or not, but I said what it felt like. I certainly didn't know if anybody else would be doing what I was doing when they tried to imitate what I was feeling. But that's all I had to offer, and I did as good a job as I could trying to describe it."

Doc took a few minutes to talk about the players he worked with, especially those who considered themselves disciples of Mr. Hogan. He talked about how surprised some of them were when they saw Mr. Hogan's swing at full speed for the first time. "Some of these guys have long, slow, flowing swings and when they saw how fast and free your swing was, quite frankly, it shocked them."

He smiled and said, "It surprised people when I was playing too."

Then Doc got specific. "I'm working with Tom Kite, who is a huge aficionado of yours," he said. "So, I cut out the passage in *Five Fundamentals* where you say that you started winning championships when you stopped trying to do a great many things perfectly."

Mr. Hogan stared straight at Doc and nodded. The quote wasn't exactly right but it was close.

Doc continued, "So, when I first read that quote to Kite,

he said, 'That can't be in there. I've read that book many times and I didn't see that.'"

"I told him, 'That's because you weren't looking for it,'" Doc said. "'You were looking for Hogan doing everything perfect.'"

"That's right," Mr. Hogan said. "You can't do a great many *difficult* things perfectly. You groove the fundamentals and then make the practice perfect."

Doc continued. "You know, Mr. Hogan, a lot of people have talked about your secret," he said. "What do you regard as your secret?"

Mr. Hogan didn't hesitate. He said, "Well, my secret, if there is one, is that I didn't start winning championships until I learned that it was okay to hit irons off the three or four tees that scared the heck out of me. For a long time I felt that in order to win big tournaments I had to attack the long, tough holes. So, I'd hit driver no matter how scary the hole was, and I'd end up making a double or triple and shoot myself out of the tournament. I came to grips with the fact that if I hit irons off those tees and just laid up to a particular spot, the worst score I was going to make on those holes was a bogey. Once I reconciled in my mind that it was okay to play those holes that way, and that bogey was not all that bad, I got comfortable and ended up making a lot more pars on those holes. I occasionally made a birdie too. But I stopped making doubles and triples. That was the secret to winning major championships, avoiding a big blowup. Unfortunately, that's not what people want to hear from me." I once asked Mr. Hogan if he ever got angry on the golf course. "It's a waste of energy," he said. He went on to say, "I only hit three or four shots a round that flew exactly as I wanted them to."

The idea that Mr. Hogan hit every drive in the middle of the fairway and every iron at the flag was a myth. On the wall at the Robert Trent Jones Club in Manassas, Virginia, and in the golf shop at Harding Park there are photos of Mr. Hogan hacking balls out of the high rough, proof that he didn't hit every shot perfectly.

There was also photographic evidence dispelling the "Wee Ice Mon" persona. This was the nickname given to him by the Scots at the British Open. It might have started out as a negative name but by the time he left Scotland, it was said with respect and immense admiration. On the wall at the Olympic Club hangs a photo of Mr. Hogan and Jack Fleck the moment after Fleck beat him in the 1955 U.S. Open, one of the greatest upsets in the game's history. He told me that loss was the biggest disappointment of his career; however, if anyone thought he wasn't a great sportsman, the photo shows otherwise. In it, Mr. Hogan can be seen giving Fleck a sincere handshake with the warmest smile imaginable. The genuine sparkle in his eyes shows that, although he wanted to win, he had a great joy for Fleck and the competition. I had seen that same look many times. One of my favorite sayings, and one I always tell my kids, is: What's worse than losing? Most people's answer is that there is nothing worse than losing, but there is. . . . Not playing at all is worse than losing.

Later, as the conversation wound down, I finally said, "Doc, are you ready to go out and play?"

He was. Mr. Hogan thanked him for coming out, and I thought Doc was going to fall over. "No, Mr. Hogan," he said. "Thank you for having me."

As usual, he waved his hand as if it were nothing.

We were barely into our round when Mr. Hogan rode out in a cart to watch us. Doc had missed the second green to the right and had a difficult pitch shot over a bunker from a tight lie. Later he told me, "I was incredibly nervous when I saw him. But it brought to mind a story Bob Toski told me years before when we were doing a golf school together in Tuscaloosa, Alabama. Before the school started the two of us went over to play Shoal Creek. As we were driving out there a couple of good old Southern boys in a truck ran us off the road, and it scared Bob to death. So we got to the first tee and Bob topped his opening tee shot. Now, I'd been playing with Bob for years and I'd never seen him mishit a shot. So I laughed and said, 'All the rounds we've played together, I've never seen you hit a shot like that.' Bob said, 'I'll tell you the last time it happened. I was an avid Hogan fan and would spend hours sitting on the tee watching Mr. Hogan hit balls. So, finally, in one event I found out I was playing in the group right in front of Hogan. On the putting green, I thought, *I hope we don't have a delay anywhere so that he catches up and sees me*. Well, somewhere in the round, there's an elevated tee with a pond in front and when we get there the group ahead has a problem. We're waiting and I see Hogan hit his second shot on the green, and I see Hogan putt and we still haven't hit. So, he finishes up and walks over and folds his arms and stands on the back of the tee. All I'm thinking is that this is the only shot in the world that matters. And I cold topped it! That was the first time I'd ever hit a shot like that in competition, and the last time I've done it until right now.' "

When Mr. Hogan came out to watch us, Doc said he thought about the Toski story and it relaxed him. He hit a great pitch shot and got it up and down. Of course, Mr. Hogan was happy for him. Dr. Bob Rotella had come to Fort Worth that day with the same mental image of Ben Hogan that most people had. He knew the mystique. By the time he left, he knew the man. And both of them seemed happier for it.

LESSONS ON THE LITTLE NINE

Mr. Hogan taught me how to hit the golf ball long, how to control the trajectory, and how to work the ball around a golf course. We practiced shaping shots into all types of winds. He taught me how to move the ball to or away from targets, but most important he taught me how to think my way around a golf course. In addition to being a master ball-striker, he was probably the best tactician who ever played, and he shared many of those tactical secrets with me as I became ready for them.

"Before you tee off on a hole you need to know what you're trying to do," he said. "You've got to start at the hole and work your way back. You should know where the hole's cut and what the green looks like. That will tell you where you want to be hitting your approach shot from and with what club. It also tells you what kind of shot you want to hit and where you want to putt from."

He told me that if a hole was cut four or five paces over a bunker and I was hitting an approach, I probably couldn't go at the hole with any club longer than a 7-iron. Anything more than that and I would have to play away from the hole, to a spot that set up the best possible putt, choosing par over the risk of bogey. To reach that point, I had to start my strategic approach at the flag and work backward. If the pin was cut on the right side of a green, then I probably wanted to hit my approach from the left side of the fairway. That might mean teeing up on the right side of the tee box to give myself the best angle, or hitting a draw from the left side of the tee. Mr. Hogan taught me to make all of these decisions before taking my first practice swing. "After you've prepared, the tournament is over. All you have to do is play."

He said that I should go home at night and think over what I'd done right and what I'd done wrong. If I did that, I could figure out where I could cut shots the next day. "After the round, you need to practice the shots that cost you.

"You have to know where you want to hit every shot and what you want to do with it," he insisted. "It's not just what line you want to hit it on, but how far, how high, and where you want it to stop.

"Always curve the ball away from trouble," he said. "If all the trouble is on the right, move it right to left, and if the trouble is on the left, move it left to right." He always wanted you to move the ball one direction or the other, even if it was only a few feet. That's how exacting he was.

This was a lot more thought than I'd ever put into a round of golf. Being young, I played the way most kids did—without much thought at all. If I was driving the ball well, I would hit driver on every par-4 and par-5, aiming for the middle and swinging as hard as I could. Sometimes I didn't know or care where a pin was cut. If I bombed my tee shot down the fairway, it wouldn't matter where the flag was tucked, or so I thought.

Mr. Hogan would grunt and frown when I said things like that. He told me, "If you aim for the middle you only have half the fairway to work with. Start it down one side or the other and you have twice as much room." Meaning, if you have a fairway that is thirty yards wide and start it down the middle, you are only working with fifteen yards on each side. If you start it down the right side and work the ball to the left, you are working with thirty yards of fairway.

"Management is as much a part of the game as hitting the ball." And he spent a great deal of time talking to me about managing my game. It wasn't enough for me to check the wind on each tee; he wanted me to check it in the parking lot before I got to the range. Mr. Hogan understood that the direction and intensity of the wind could completely change the complexion of a golf course. In planning a round, you had to know how the wind was going to affect your strategy.

Ken Venturi tells a great story about Mr. Hogan's constant

awareness of his environment. Mr. Venturi played as many rounds with Mr. Hogan as he could, and always asked questions when they were together. During several practice rounds at Augusta National, Mr. Venturi noticed that Mr. Hogan took more time than normal to hit his approach shots into the par-4 11th and to hit his tee shots at the par-3 12th. When Mr. Venturi asked him about it, Mr. Hogan said, "It's the wind." Then he pointed to the flag at 11 and the flag at 12, which aren't that far apart. They were blowing in opposite directions.

"You can't go by what you see," Mr. Hogan told him. "You have to go by what you feel." If he was standing in the 11th fairway, the flag might be down, but if he could feel the wind, he knew it was blowing at treetop level and he would play his approach shot accordingly. The same was true on 12. When Mr. Venturi asked him why he'd stood over the ball so long on the 12th tee, Mr. Hogan patted the side of his face and said, "I won't hit it until I feel the wind on my cheek. That's when I know what it's doing."

Along with the management lessons were swing lessons. He was always having me experiment, but there were some common themes that never changed. He wanted me to keep my arms close together. To make that point, he would take off his belt and strap it around my elbows so that the width of my arms would never vary during the swing. This was a standard drill for him, and one he showed to many of his friends. It was also a precursor to many swing aids on the market today. The next time you see a Swing Connection device with Velcro and colorful straps, remember that Mr. Hogan achieved the same thing with a leather belt from Leonard's.

As far back as I can remember he would have me brace against my right knee, which helped with stability in my backswing. He felt like his right knee moved minimally on the way back, and by bracing against it, his hips and torso would turn correctly, putting himself in position for the proper sequence in the downswing: hips, shoulders, arms, hands, and last, the head. He would often tell me to look at the ball a little longer so that I would keep my head behind the ball through impact.

Another common theme was swing plane. He wanted my left arm lower in my back swing to produce a flatter, more circular motion. This creates a path for the shaft to return to its original address position. He felt the better you could simulate your address position at impact, the more consistent you would become. If you look at pictures of him from down the line at address and impact, the angle of the shaft is almost identical.

Every lesson included "Hit it harder!" He always accused me of "lollygagging," which meant, to him, that I wasn't swinging hard enough. Of course, wouldn't anyone look like they were "lollygagging" next to him? *Lollygag* and *coolakwachy* (his made-up word for "rear end"), were two of his favorite words.

He demonstrated a favorite concept by putting a shaft in between my forearms in an attempt to get my shoulders and arms in what he thought was the correct position. He would put the shaft under my left forearm, forcing the left arm up while pushing the right elbow down and close to my side. It was awkward and impossible to achieve. It must have felt to him like he had his right elbow much lower than his left arm at address. In other words, he thought if you were standing behind him looking down the line of the shot, you would see his whole left arm. When I watched him, though, his right arm completely blocked out the view of his left, so one day I asked if I could videotape his swing, thinking I could show him what he actually did. He agreed, but when I asked him if he wanted to take a look, he had no interest in doing so.

"I know what it feels like. I don't need to see it."

I assume that these are the last recorded images of him hitting balls, since this was after he did the commercial at Riviera.

He drew analogies from other sports when teaching. "Who was the best hitter in the history of baseball?" he asked. I wasn't much of a baseball fan. In fact, I'm not much of a sports fan at all. My husband loves when I meet professional athletes, because then I have a personal interest and a reason to watch games with him. When he wants me to watch a sporting event, he'll give me a human-interest story about someone on his team to get me hooked. Beyond that, I couldn't care less what teams are playing or who wins. I sat next to Heisman Trophy winner Tim Brown on a flight in the mid-nineties. It wasn't that he was a handsome, athletic-looking man that caught my eye (although he certainly was that), it was the book he was reading, *Men Are from Mars, Women Are from Venus.* Suddenly I had to know how he came to be reading that book. When dinner came, I couldn't hold my curiosity any longer.

"Did you pick that up on your own, or did your wife pick that out for you?" I asked him, pointing to the book.

He smiled and said, "I've been in two serious relationships in my life and they both ended. Finally, I had to look in the mirror and realize I was the only constant."

We talked for the rest of the flight. When we started sharing war stories about our respective injuries, he actually had to explain to me what a wide receiver did so I would understand how he'd gotten hurt. Tim and I had a great conversation and I liked him instantly. The book must have helped as well. A year later, he got married.

So, needless to say, when Mr. Hogan asked me who the best hitter in baseball was, I didn't know. He stared at me with those piercing blue eyes for a few seconds until it was clear that I couldn't answer.

"Ted Williams!" he said, as if it were the most obvious thing in the world. Then he took a long iron out of his bag, held it up over his shoulder like a baseball bat, and swung it two or three times as if he were hitting a baseball. As little as I knew, I could tell that it was a pretty good baseball swing. "Now watch as I go a little lower," Mr. Hogan said, bending slightly at the waist. "And lower," he said as he went fully into his stance. Without any noticeable change in the mechanics of the swing, his Ted Williams baseball motion morphed into his golf swing.

"If your arms are close together, and you start the downswing by turning your hips, the club will move inside on the perfect plane, and you can hit it with your right hand as hard as you want."

"The right hand," I said, making sure that I understood.

"Yes, the right hand. Did I stutter?"

"Mumble. You don't stutter, you mumble," I said.

One day he was mumbling something under his breath. I said, "Hey, I heard that. If you're going to insult me, do it so I can hear you."

He said, "I've tried but it can't be done."

"What can't be done?" I asked.

"I can't seem to insult you!"

That's how it was with us. For the first few minutes, we were nice to each other and then the banter would start. One day we were standing there insulting each other and he started laughing. "You're the damnedest thing I've ever seen. I don't think I've ever had a friend like you."

The golf pro at Shady Oaks described my relationship with Mr. Hogan as being like "a playfully antagonistic granddaughter." That was as good a description as any. A lot of people wonder, if we were so close, why I always called him Mr. Hogan and still refer to him so formally to this day. He didn't want me doing it. In fact, he told me several times, "Would you please call me Ben!" But I couldn't do it. I was raised to call my elders Mr. and Mrs. and it just didn't feel right.

That formality didn't stop me from giving Mr. Hogan a hard time, however. One day I got after him about smoking. "Those things are bad for you," I said.

"Worst thing in the world," he answered back.

"They'll kill you, and I want you around for a while. I'm not done with you yet."

"How long have I been working with you?" he asked.

"About five years."

"Five years!" he exclaimed. "You've got to be kidding me!"

"Five of the best years of your life."

"Five of the worst. Can't you figure out anything for yourself?"

"Mr. Hogan, I think God put you on this earth specifically so I didn't have to figure anything out for myself." I got a good laugh out of him with that one!

Another time he came out while I was practicing and started with "You know, they charge me four dollars an hour for a cart to come out here. You're only worth two."

I remember thinking, *They charge him for a cart?*

After I had hit all my balls and was heading out to pick them up, I asked him, "Are you going to be here when I get back?"

"I hope so," he quipped.

Those were normal conversations for us. But there were times when we were serious too. I remember coming home after having a good tournament and telling him that I owed him so much and that there was no way I could ever pay him back for all he'd done.

"You don't owe me a thing," he said. Then he added, "I've had my career. Now I'm enjoying yours."

My father, who never shied away from offering his opinions, continued to caddy for me six to eight times a year when I was first on tour. During one of my tournaments, he had been telling me I needed to develop a pre-shot routine. "A what?" I asked. This was long before most people understood the importance of a consistent pre-shot routine. But Dad had read about it somewhere and was determined that I needed to come up with one. One of his favorite sayings is "I may not always be right but I never think I'm wrong." In other words, he harped on it all week and then finished his argument with "Ask Mr. Hogan. See if he has a pre-shot routine."

The next time I was out at Shady Oaks I got in a cart and waved as I rode past the bay window, where Mr. Hogan was sitting at his table. I never asked him to come out. I just let him know I was there and he would show up. I guess if he hadn't shown up I would have gone looking for him, but I never needed to do that. People would later tell me that I was the only person he would jump up from his table for and run outside to see. When he came out that day, I was at my usual spot on the Little Nine, hitting 8-iron shots toward an oak tree near the creek that meandered through the property. We chatted for a few minutes about the tournament and then we got down to business. He watched in silence for a couple of minutes. Then I said, "Mr. Hogan, do you have a pre-shot routine?"

"What's that?" he asked.

"Do you do the same thing every time before every shot?"

"No," he grumbled. "You hit the ball when you're ready. If you're ready quick, you hit it quick. If you're not ready, you take more time."

I smiled and went back to my practice session, satisfied that I'd disproved one of Dad's theories. But as we practiced, I noticed that he actually did have a pre-shot routine. On every shot, he held the club in his right hand and then switched it to his left hand while he looked at the target. Then he would check his grip and waggle the club behind the ball as he took his stance. He would step in with his right foot first, and then his left. One more waggle and one more look at the target, then with a slight kicking in of the right knee, he would move into his swing. He did it with every club and he did it every time. His routine had a cadence to it. He even shifted his feet in his stance the same number of times (four each) on every shot. He didn't know he had a pre-shot routine, but he had one of the most consistent ones in the game.

I learned from listening to him and I learned from watching him. In our conversations, he would paint such vivid pictures, it felt like I was watching him play in his prime.

During the 1953 British Open, which Mr. Hogan won in his only Open appearance, the par-5, 6th hole at Carnoustie became legendary. He drove the ball onto a narrow sliver of land between an out-of-bounds fence and a row of bunkers every day. He played the hole three under for the week, and that small strip of hard ground was forever known as Hogan's Alley.

"Everyone wants to talk about the 6th at Carnoustie, when I hit my tee shot down the left side. The wind was blowing hard left to right. I knew I could start it down that fence line on the left and the wind would keep it in bounds. It's not like there was no ground there. It was probably twenty yards wide. In the U.S. Open, that's the average width of a fairway. It was just because of the out-of-bounds and deep bunkers that people thought it was something special. If it had been rough on both sides, nobody would have thought twice about me hitting it there every day."

"But it was out of bounds on the left," I said.

"Yeah, but that's not where I was hitting it. It didn't matter what was over there. I was shaping the shot away from the stakes."

He often used Augusta National for examples of course management that he shared with me. "Everybody thought Augusta was a course where you had to move the ball from right to left, but that's not true," he said. "A fade works just fine."

"What about thirteen?" I asked, referring to the dogleg left par-5, where every player tries to draw the ball around the corner.

He shook his head. "That tree at the corner is the perfect line. Start it there with a slight fade. The ball will still bounce left and you're in great shape." Of course, that tree is now a mature Georgian pine and that opening is continuing to narrow.

I loved listening to him recount why he hit the ball in certain spots. It was almost like getting a virtual playing lesson at Augusta. He used the downhill par-4 9th as an example of playing for your lie. Mr. Hogan believed that it was better to have a longer shot from a level lie in the fairway than it was to have a short shot from an uneven lie. For that reason, he said he never tried to hit the ball as hard as he could off the 9th tee. Even though most players tried to hit a big slinging hook to use the downhill slope of the fairway for extra yardage, Mr. Hogan chose to fade his tee shot to a plateau on the right side, a flat spot not much bigger than the size of my living room.

"From there you have a level lie and a perfect look at the green," he said. "It doesn't matter where they cut the hole, I can get to it from that spot."

He also used the 9th to make the point that it didn't matter how far you hit a particular club. The important thing was how you executed the shot you were trying to hit. For example, a shot from 155 yards in benign conditions would have been a 6-iron shot for him when we were practicing and playing together, and probably a 7-iron during his prime. But if he had a 155-yard shot in a round, he might hit anything from a 4-iron to a 7-iron, depending on the conditions and what he was trying to do. That was why, unlike a lot of pros today, Mr. Hogan never asked me how far I hit a particular club.

One story he told typified this philosophy. Everyone knew that Mr. Hogan and Sam Snead were fierce competitors, but they were also friends. They would call each other for outings and exhibition business, and they often appeared in promotions together. But on the golf course there was nothing friendly about the games they played. Even when they got to the "exhibition" stages of their careers, the pride and satisfaction of winning was worth more than any prize money, especially against each other. One of the greatest episodes of *Shell's Wonderful World of Golf* was a May 1964 match between Mr. Hogan and Sam Snead at Houston Country Club. It was a television show, so the time span between shots was up to twenty minutes, as the production crew had to move cameras. Mr. Hogan prepared meticulously, as he would for any tour event. He played several practice rounds and mapped out a detailed strategy for the course. He hit fourteen fairways and eighteen greens, shooting 69 to beat Snead. Afterward, Gene Sarazen, who narrated the show, called Mr. Hogan's effort "one of the finest rounds of golf [he'd] ever seen."

They were different men with very different styles, and Snead was well-known for peeking into his opponents' bags to see what clubs they were hitting. Mr. Hogan couldn't have cared less what his fellow competitors hit. The practice of looking into another player's bag is not against the rules, and yet when players do it, they do so with utmost discretion. Maybe we (players) see it as a sign of weakness. According to Mr. Hogan, Snead was the exception. "You'd barely have the club out of the bag before he'd be poking around to see what club you had," Mr. Hogan said. "On the 9th hole at Augusta, I was down there near the flat spot, and had a slight wind in my face, so I took out a 5-iron and cut it in there just under the hole to about ten feet. Sam was right there looking in my bag. He goes over to hit his shot, and I didn't look, but I figured he must have pulled a 5-iron too, because the ball was still rising as it went over the green. Looking in my bag let him know what I'd hit, but he didn't know how I'd hit it."

Mr. Hogan could land the ball on the same spot with three different clubs. He played by feel. He always stressed hitting the right shot for the situation. He might feather a soft shot in from left to right for a front pin on a firm green or hit a low rolling shot to a back pin so he could eliminate the possibility of flying it over a green. He figured if it went over, it wouldn't be by much.

He told me stories about his practice rounds and the money games they would play. "We used to play nassau games, but I rarely won them because I never hit at a pin during a practice round. If they had the pin in a certain spot during a practice round, it sure wasn't going to be there in the tournament."

He won plenty of games during other rounds, though.

Mr. Hogan and Claude Harmon would play a points game where you got one point for hitting the fairway, one for hitting the green, one for a birdie, one for winning the hole, and you lost one for a three-putt. At fifty bucks a point, the games could get pricey if you weren't hitting it well.

"We'd play that game at Seminole and Claude would hit driver five or six more times than I would. I hit 4-wood off the tee a lot there. Finally, he said to me, 'Ben, why do you hit 4-wood here? There's no trouble.' I told him that 4-wood left me with the club I wanted to hit into the green, and driver would put me too close."

"What do you mean by too close? You're pretty good with your wedges. Why wouldn't you get as close as possible?"

"There's more to it than just hitting it far!" He would get adamant with me and say, "Sometimes hitting 2-iron or 4-wood would leave me with a full shot or a better angle into a green. Plus, the fairway gets narrower the further down you go. I'd beaten him out of fifty bucks almost every day by hitting that fairway. Claude hit a lot more 4-woods after that."

He always said the tee shot was the most important shot because it set you up for the hole. "You need to think ahead so you know what shot you want into the green then you can set it up with your tee shot."

I loved the playing lessons. More than anything, he taught me about hitting the proper shot for the situation. It was something he always stressed, but he would also concede that sometimes you just couldn't fight your eye. Meaning, if a shot looked to you like it needed to be hit one direction or another it was very hard to go against that. Sometimes you had to go with the shot that felt right.

We would go out on the course and practice hitting all kinds of shots. He would take me to a hard part of ground and have me take half swings, making sure I thumped the ground in the same spot and with the same level of force every time.

"Thump the ground! Thump the ground!" he would say. It reminded me of my ballet teacher when I was growing up. She used to yell at me to keep going when my legs felt like jelly and I would somehow find a way to do it. By having me thump the ground with short swings time after time, he was conditioning me to make solid contact and helping me develop lag in my downswing, which would put the speed in the proper place. Mr. Hogan believed that if you could get your club head moving faster after the ball, you would hit it farther and straighter.

He talked quite a bit about hitting the ball with the right hand. "As long as your hips are out of the way and you're coming from the inside into the back of the ball, you hit it with the right hand. When I was playing, I wished I'd had three right hands so I could hit it harder." Then he demonstrated by taking his left hand off and swinging the club. But he only held it with the bottom three fingers of the right hand. When he talked about hitting it with the right hand, he meant the bottom three fingers, and the speed through the hitting area with those three fingers was impressive.

We worked on all different kinds of lies. He taught me that a shot off an uphill lie, especially into the wind, tended to flair upward and left, but that by weakening my left hand grip and abbreviating my finish, I could hold the clubface angle through impact and that would produce a lower, straighter shot. He would have me hit shots from a lie with the ball above my feet, and he taught me that it wouldn't go as much left and would also go the correct distance if I started with my clubface open. We would drive around the course and find different shots to practice. One might require a little fade, and the next, a high draw. "There's not enough time in the day to practice all the shots," he would say.

I was thumbing through a magazine one day, wishing for the tan feet on one of those unrealistic beauties, when Kirk looked over my shoulder and said, "Yeah, but she doesn't have the high draw shot. . . ." Thanks, Mr. Hogan.

I didn't realize at the time how different all those lessons on the Little Nine were from his practice sessions in his prime, when he would hit balls alone and not speak to anyone for hours. I was a running commentary for us and had something to say after every shot when we were practicing. If he was hitting, my comments would sound something like this:

"Oh, that one looked good."

"Nice shot."

"That was the best one today."

"What did you have for dinner last night?"

"How did that one feel?"

He would smile and nod and give the occasional "That's got it." Or, "Steak and potatoes."

If I was hitting, I would be saying things like:

"That felt good. How did that look?"

"I didn't like that one. What did I do wrong?"

"I've got a psychology test tomorrow and I'm not looking forward to it."

"Oops. You didn't like that shot, did you?"

So many times I would hit one, turn around to look at him, and before I would say anything, he would tell me where I had hit the ball. He couldn't see it but the combination of the swing and the sound told him exactly where it had gone and how it had gotten there. It always amazed me how he did that. "Are you sure you're not lying to me about your eyesight?"

There were times when we got down to business, but when I think of our time on the Little Nine I remember laughter. He knew I was always serious when I was hitting a shot but before and after we would be laughing about something.

MONDAY LUNCHES AND
THE REST OF THE STORY

Although I mostly saw a lighthearted side of him I had also witnessed the side that earned him his reputation. Almost everyone who knew Mr. Hogan has a cranky curmudgeon story about him, but some of those stories end with a twist. They end with Mr. Hogan engaging in some act of unexpected kindness, like helping someone in need or standing up for someone who couldn't stand up for themselves. Others resulted from his dry sense of humor being misinterpreted.

A lot of these tales took place at Shady Oaks, where people walked around him with a certain sense of trepidation. One day, as he was hitting drivers from the 18th tee across the Little Nine and into the rough on the right side of the 11th fairway, one of the members named Ed Baker hit his tee shot on 11 into the right rough where all of Mr. Hogan's practice balls had landed. Naturally, Mr. Baker picked up and looked at a few of Mr. Hogan's balls while looking for his own.

"Is that Ed Baker?" he asked me. "Is he stealing my balls?"

"No, Mr. Hogan," I said. "I think he's just looking for his tee shot."

Before I could finish my explanation, Mr. Hogan had teed up a ball and hit it right at Mr. Baker. The ball landed a yard to the right of him, sending Mr. Baker high-stepping backward.

Mr. Baker hopped in his cart and rode over to where we were hitting. "Ben, are you trying to hit me?" he said.

"Are you trying to steal my balls?" Mr. Hogan replied.

"I was just looking for my tee shot," Mr. Baker said.

Mr. Hogan grunted and went back to his practice, leaving Mr. Baker and me both to wonder if he'd actually been trying to hit him, or if he'd been aiming one yard to the right. Now that I think about it, that might have been how he got the Ultra mixed in with his shag balls. Ed never found his ball that day.

Things could get equally tense indoors. Mr. Hogan's table in the grillroom—the largest round table in any of the regular dining rooms, with a lazy Susan in the middle—was like the court of King Arthur, with all the politics and posturing you might expect. He always sat with his back to the rest of the diners. This served two purposes: to insulate him from gawkers and to give him a panoramic view of the 9th and 18th holes. There was also a button on the column next to him that looked like the call button for a dumbwaiter. It was a call button all right, Mr. Hogan's call button for whenever he needed anything. One push and the staff came running.

There was no clear-cut protocol for who got to sit at the table, and no one could ever make sense of the seating arrangements. Scores of people claim to have sat at Mr. Hogan's side, and I'm sure plenty of men graced the table over the years. As long as you were polite and didn't talk his ear off, he didn't mind having lunch with you, and plenty of people took advantage. But there were rules. One of the men who sat at Mr. Hogan's side was oil and gas geologist Bob Wynn. The two had a good friendship because they were very much alike, quiet and serious men with big hearts, a love of the game, and a taste for good wine. Plus, Mr. Hogan had a number of oil investments in Texas and he enjoyed picking Bob's brain about the science of wildcatting.

Bob also kept the gate at Mr. Hogan's table. For example, one afternoon when a new member plopped down at the table and ordered, Mr. Hogan quietly got up and walked into the locker room. Sensing something was wrong, Bob followed him into the locker room.

"Bob, who's that fellow at the table?" Mr. Hogan asked.

"He's one of the new members," Bob said. "I haven't met him."

"Well, go tell him to either properly introduce himself or go eat somewhere else."

Bob did just that, spending a couple of uncomfortable moments explaining to the new member that Mr. Hogan was a stickler for protocol, and if he chose not to formally introduce himself, then he would perhaps be happier dining elsewhere. The man was first stunned, and then angry, and finally embarrassed. When Mr. Hogan returned to the table a few minutes later, the man jumped up, extended his hand, and said, "Mr. Hogan, I'm so sorry I didn't introduce myself earlier." Mr. Hogan acted as if it were nothing, and the rest of the afternoon went by without incident.

Even those who were regulars lived with the slightly irrational fear that they might one day be banished. One afternoon, with the table full of regulars, Mr. Hogan sat quietly in his chair and scribbled a note of some sort. Nobody asked him what he was doing. If he didn't volunteer to share those details, most people knew better than to ask. After he finished, he reached into his pocket and pulled out five hundred-dollar bills and stuffed them into an envelope along with the note. Everyone watched but no one said a word. Then Mr. Hogan passed the envelope to Bob Wynn and said, "Pass this around and have everybody put at least a hundred in there."

He never said what the money was for, and nobody at the table asked. But everyone dug through their wallets or borrowed cash from friends to meet Mr. Hogan's hundred-dollar minimum. The envelope came back full, and without a word he sealed it, put it in his back pocket, and continued with his lunch. The money turned out to be for an uninsured waitress at the club who had a child in the hospital. Nobody at the table that day knew what they had contributed to, but they all left with a classic Mr. Hogan story, one they valued far more than the contributions they had made to an anonymous worthy cause.

It's funny that only the adults hovered in apprehension around his table. It was nothing for him to walk over to the window and make faces at children who walked past. One summer day a member's twin three-year-olds walked by after an afternoon at the pool, and Mr. Hogan hopped up, pressed his nose against the glass, stuck his thumbs in his ears, flared his fingers like antlers, and stuck out his tongue. Of course the children laughed and mimicked him, having no idea who the silly man was making faces at them. Then he returned to the table, and the parents probably told their children never to forget that funny man.

Like everything else in his life, the table took on a mystique. No one sat there without him, and people would bring guests into the grill just to show them Mr. Hogan's table as if it were a museum piece. It's still in the grillroom, even though the clubhouse has been completely remodeled and the rest of the furnishings replaced. Mr. Hogan's table, like his lockers and his clubs and his shag bag, has been preserved like a shrine. For him, it was just a comfortable place to watch the comings and goings on the golf course. I spent some time there, although I was also a party to some table controversy one afternoon.

Monday was the slowest day at the club. The clubhouse wasn't closed, but the restaurant didn't serve and if the maintenance crew needed to conduct major operations on the course, Monday was the day. None of that slowed Mr. Hogan down. He kept to his routine, arriving at the club no later than lunchtime, sitting at the table, and going out to practice with me if the weather permitted. He always insisted on shagging his own balls, and his shag bag looked more like a bowling ball bag to me. He never used a picker nor did he flip the balls into the bag with a wedge. He bent down and picked every one up individually, standing erect to put each ball in the bag. Sometimes his balls were so close together he could have picked several up at a time, but that was not part of his routine.

Inviting me into the men's grill for lunch on Mondays was part of our ritual. Since there was no food service Mr. Hogan brought the meal, although calling it lunch was a stretch. He brought one banana and a pack of peanut butter crackers, which he insisted on splitting with me. It was barely enough food to keep a bird alive, but he would faithfully pull out a butter knife, wipe it down until it was operating-room clean, and cut the banana in half while giving me three of the six crackers in the pack. Sometimes I would make chocolate chip cookies to add to our fare.

"When I went to the British Open in 1953, Valerie and I both took sandwiches out to the course every day," he told me one Monday in the middle of this routine. "But my caddy looked like he hadn't had a decent meal since before the war. There were still a lot of hungry people over there, even though the war had been over for nearly ten years. I felt so sorry for the fellow that I gave him half my sandwich every day at lunchtime. He would thank me like it was the only thing he'd eaten in a week. He ate my candy too."

"Your candy?" I asked.

"Yes, I kept a bag of candy in my bag for energy late in the day. This fellow got so nervous he ate every bit of it. So, late in the week I took two bags and said to him, 'This is your bag, and this is my bag. Now, don't eat out of my bag.'"

I laughed, because it was just so typical of the way he did things.

"After it was over, and we were on the ship heading home, Valerie and I got to talking, and we realized that she'd given that caddy half of her sandwich every day too. So we were both eating half a sandwich, and the caddy was eating a whole one. He made out better than we did."

"Didn't you get into some kind of trouble with the press over there about your room?" I asked. This was a story I'd heard in bits and pieces. In the pre-Internet days, there was no quick way of researching something like that, so I asked the source.

"It was terrible what they wrote," he said, shaking his head. "We got over there and there was one little hotel in the entire town. Now remember, I had to qualify for the tournament just like everybody else. I'd won the Masters and U.S. Open, but I still had to qualify at a little course called Panmure."

"Never heard of it," I said.

"There's a reason. They had to herd the sheep off before we played. Anyway, I had to play thirty-six holes of qualifying, then the practice rounds, and then the tournament itself, and when we got there the one little hotel in town didn't have a private bathroom. The one bathroom they had didn't have a tub. I had to soak my legs or I wouldn't have made it. I looked at that bathroom and said to Valerie, 'Let's just go home.' Valerie got on the phone and called some fellow who'd given her his card. Next thing I know another fellow showed up and said, 'Mr. Hogan, I'm your driver, here to take you to your house in Dundee.' It was a nice place with a tub, not too far from the course. I didn't have anything to do with getting that place, but I knew I couldn't stay in the hotel in town. The press had a time with us over that."

"Why didn't you say something?" I asked.

"Let people believe what they want to believe," he would say.

"But how do you stand it?" I asked. "I would hate if people were thinking bad things about me, especially if they weren't true!"

He figured if people were going to say negative things about him, it wouldn't do any good to try to correct them. I loved hearing those and other stories during our Monday indoor picnics. He told me once about a pro-am he had committed to playing, but as he was flying in for the event, the plane had to be diverted because of weather. They had two botched landings at a second airport away from the town where he was supposed to be, and by the time he got on the ground, word had spread that he'd been a no-show for the pro-am.

"Why didn't you tell them what happened?" I asked.

"If they want to think the worst about me, let them think it," he said.

One of the greatest examples of his not setting the record straight is what I refer to as the "Call Mr. Dunlap" story. Someone had told me this story but it didn't quite ring true, so I asked him about it one day.

The short version goes like this: Gary Player wanted to ask Mr. Hogan a question about the golf swing, so he called him. According to the story, Mr. Hogan asked him what clubs he played, and when Gary said, "Dunlap," Mr. Hogan said, "Then why don't you call Mr. Dunlap?" And with that, he hung up the phone.

That story burnished the image of Mr. Hogan as a loner, a man who didn't give back. "Was it true?" I asked. He pinned me with one of his stares and it lasted long enough to make me a little uncomfortable. I think he was trying to decide if he wanted to tell me the rest of the story.

Finally he quietly said, "Well, there was a little more to the story."

The first thing that never gets told is that Gary called him in the middle of the night. Jarring someone out of a sound sleep is certainly a reason to expect a snippy response. But that wasn't the biggest problem. The real reason for Mr. Hogan's reply was the fact that years earlier, Mr. Hogan had given Gary a driver along with his telephone number if he ever needed anything. The next day he saw Gary with that driver, but Gary had painted it black to make it look like the clubs he was representing at the time.

"Why haven't you ever told your side of the story?" I asked.

He shrugged and said, "Didn't see any reason to make a fuss over it. Player's made a living telling it. No need to get in the way of that."

This was typical of the way he thought. If it came down to a choice between setting the record straight and looking like he was spinning something to his own advantage, or remaining quiet and letting people think whatever they wanted, he always opted for the latter.

An old story has been told for years about his leaving a golf tournament that he had won in Denver before the award's presentation. The press skewered him, saying he was too important to hang around and thank the very people who were putting food on his table. The local papers also wrote that he had blown off some kids seeking autographs. Historians and sensational biographers have used that story as an example of Mr. Hogan's didn't-care-what-others-thought attitude. The problem was, it wasn't true.

"I had played so badly in the final round that I was sure I was out of contention," he told me. "Golf wasn't on television in those days, so the leaders weren't in the final group. I finished early, looked at the board, did the math, and left. I was all the way to Salt Lake City when Valerie heard that I'd won. Well, I'll tell you, that was as embarrassed as I've ever been. I called the president of the Denver Civic Golf Association—they were the sponsor—and explained what happened. I apologized and asked him to pass along my deepest thanks to everyone."

The expression on his face told me that it still bothered him decades later.

"As for the other stuff, there was one young fellow who jumped out and asked for an autograph as I was walking off the seventh green. I told him I'd be happy to sign it after the round. Just wait for me to finish. Somehow it got sensationalized."

Every player I know does the same thing. If you stop for one there will always be others.

I had become pretty comfortable in the men's grill on Mondays. Women weren't allowed in there, but since we were the only people around, no one seemed to care. Then a new manager noticed. That day when I sat down for my typical seventy-five-calorie lunch with Mr. Hogan, the phone rang and one of the staff called me over.

It was the new manager.

"You cannot be in the men's grill," he said.

"I know," I said. "But it's only on Mondays and Mr. Hogan asked me to join him."

"No, *you* don't understand," he said. "You are not allowed in the men's grill under any circumstances, no matter what day it is or who asked you."

I said one of the quickest "yes, sirs" of my life. The last thing I wanted was to get on the naughty list at Shady Oaks. When I walked back to the table, I said, "Mr. Hogan, I better get going."

"What do you mean?" he said. "We haven't had lunch yet."

"I know, but I really need to get out and practice." It was a terrible attempt to skirt the awkward moment. I didn't want to tell him what had happened, because I knew it would make matters worse. "I'll see you out there."

My lame excuses didn't fly with Mr. Hogan. I got the sense

that he knew something was wrong, even though we never discussed the incident again. Maybe it was a coincidence, but a week later, that manager was no longer working with the club, and the next Monday I joined Mr. Hogan as usual.

I often heard people speak about the harsh, uncompromising man who once scrapped an entire shipment of clubs from his new factory because they didn't meet his exacting standards. But I always saw him as someone who simply insisted that things be right. If you were genuine and well-meaning, he would be incredibly accommodating. If you were trying to use him for some personal advantage, he would have nothing to do with you.

That's what happened when Nick Faldo came to Shady Oaks to visit him. Mr. Hogan had no problem with Faldo; in fact, the two men sat at his table and talked about golf for a long time. But according to those who were there, the man who brought Nick out that day behaved as though he and Mr. Hogan were best buddies. As a result, Mr. Hogan ignored him. And when the man asked Mr. Hogan if he wanted to come out and watch Faldo hit some shots, Mr. Hogan said, "No, I think I'll stay here."

An hour or so later, another member of Faldo's entourage came in and said, "Mr. Hogan, we would really love it if you came out and watched Nick."

All photos courtesy of the author unless credited.

Here I am with Mr. Hogan outside the clubhouse at Shady Oaks in 1985.

Left: This is Mr. Hogan teasing me about the golf swing he helped me create. Charles, the head waiter, snapped it after we got the Christmas picture.

Below: In the Men's Grill at Shady Oaks in 1988. My brothers and I wanted to get a Christmas picture for our parents.

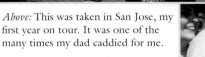

Above: This was taken in San Jose, my first year on tour. It was one of the many times my dad caddied for me.

Right: A shot from the U.S. Open in 1991 when Mr. Hogan came out to watch me play in my final round.

Bob Straus

Left: With Mr. and Mrs. Hogan at the reception that Shady Oaks threw for me after I won my first tournament in Minneapolis.

Below: At the Dinah Shore with my mom and brother Eric. He spent a couple summers caddying for me in the early nineties and he still loves coming out to tournaments.

Left: Here's another shot from the same event. Finally, I got a picture of us where I'm not wearing golf clothes.

This is a swing sequence from the 1989 video I found.
I asked Mr. Hogan if I could tape his swing and, amazingly, he let me. I'm pretty sure this is the last time his swing was ever caught on film.

This is a second swing sequence from that 1989 video—
this time with a front view of Mr. Hogan's swing.

This is a photo from the same video and it reminds me of
all those days we spent together.

Mr. Hogan nodded and stayed in his seat. I guess he was affirming that he understood how much they wanted him to watch Faldo, but he was quite comfortable where he was, and had no intention of moving. Again, this was no reflection on Faldo. Mr. Hogan admired Nick's work ethic and his tactical approach to the game.

Mr. Hogan could make a point using very few words. When Tom Byrum was practicing and playing out at Shady Oaks during his early years on tour, Mr. Hogan worked with Tom and helped him with his equipment. One day Tom's car was in the shop, so he stayed home in the morning taking care of business matters while waiting for his car to be fixed. It was well into the afternoon by the time he got to the club. When Mr. Hogan walked out to the Little Nine to watch him, Tom had only hit five or six shots, a fact made plain by the small number of divots near the balls.

"Did you just get here?" Mr. Hogan asked him.

"Yes, sir," Tom said. "My car was in the shop this morning."

Mr. Hogan stood silently while Tom hit three or four balls. Then he said, "Where do you live?"

Tom began to sweat. He sensed where this was going. He gave Mr. Hogan his address, which was about two miles from the club.

That led to another long silence as Tom hit five or six more balls. Then Mr. Hogan said, "Do you own a bicycle?"

At that point Tom wanted to crawl in a hole. But he manned up and said, "Yes, sir, I own a bicycle."

More silence and three balls later, Mr. Hogan said, "Your house is only two miles from here. You could have walked, couldn't you?"

Tom wanted to do whatever it took for this to be over so Mr. Hogan would move on to helping him with his swing. "Yes, sir, I guess I could have walked," he said.

He hit about three more balls and finally got the courage to look up and see the expression on Mr. Hogan's face. He couldn't see it. Mr. Hogan had turned, wordlessly, and was walking back to the clubhouse. The lesson was over for the day.

Mr. Hogan could also be the most accommodating person in the world. I asked him to sign dozens of photos and prints for friends and charities, and he never once said no, because he understood how important those things were to people who would never get the chance to meet him. However, those of us who did know him were judicious in our requests. Like everything else in his life, he was meticulous with his signature. A friend of mine met him once in his office at the Ben Hogan Company and surprised Mr. Hogan by pulling out a glossy print of the 1-iron shot at Merion. "Mr. Hogan, I brought this picture and I was hoping you would sign it for me."

For the next five seconds my friend was treated to the unblinking stare. "It felt like it lasted a year," he said.

Finally, Mr. Hogan said, "Okay." He retreated behind his desk, where he laid the print out and smoothed the edges. Then he opened the top drawer of his desk, took out a tissue, and wiped the print clean. Once he was sure there were no smudges or imperfections on the surface, Mr. Hogan opened another drawer and took out a small note tablet and a felt-tip marker and practiced his signature twice on paper before signing the print.

"No wonder he didn't sign many autographs," my friend said to me later. "He wouldn't have had time to do anything else."

The people at Shady Oaks did their best to protect him from intrusive autograph seekers or people who simply wanted to rub elbows with a legend. My brothers and I were among those who told our friends, "Look, we'll take you out there, but we're not going to run up to Mr. Hogan and ask him to pose for pictures. If he speaks to us, we'll speak to him, but we're not going to impose on the man's time."

Still, when the time was right he could always strike the perfect chord. One quiet afternoon when almost no one else was at the club, a young couple and their four rambunctious kids walked into the golf shop. "Well, kids, this is it," the father said with a dramatic sweep of his arms. "This is where he is. He comes here every day."

When the golf shop attendant asked if he could help them, the father said, "Yes, yes, we're the Rosmelds from Pinewood,

Minnesota, and we've driven down here on our vacation to meet Ben Hogan and get him to autograph our book," he said, waving his copy of *Five Lessons* like an evangelical minister professing the Word.

"Ah, it doesn't work that way," the shop assistant said. "We don't bother Mr. Hogan."

"Yes, but this is our vacation," the man said. "We've driven all the way down here just for this."

By this time the Rosmeld kids were clanging putters on the display racks and bouncing on the furniture.

"Let me go back and see if he's here," the shop assistant said.

Of course, Mr. Hogan was there. When the situation was explained to him, Mr. Hogan grumbled for a second and said, "Write down his name and bring the book back here."

The assistant went back into the shop and told Mr. Rosmeld to print his name on a piece of paper, hand over the book, and keep the kids from tearing the place apart while he went to the back one more time.

Mr. Hogan took the book and the paper with Rosmeld's name, and after a few deliberative minutes he wrote a wonderful inscription in which he expressed what a great pleasure it was to have the likes of Mr. Rosmeld as a fan.

Back in the golf shop, the assistant handed Rosmeld his book and stood in amazement as the man read the inscription with tears in his eyes. Even the kids stared at Mr. Hogan's signature as if it were some ancient magical inscription. They left for Pinewood, Minnesota, having experienced the thrill of their lives, with their own Hogan story.

On another occasion, one of my brother's mini-tour friends wanted an autographed scorecard, which Mike got with no problem, but when the same friend came to Fort Worth to visit, he wanted an introduction. That wasn't quite so simple. "We'll go out there and if it happens, it happens, but we're not making a big deal out of it," Mike said.

His friend was beside himself with excitement. When they arrived at Shady Oaks, Mr. Hogan was sitting in his normal spot. "Look, he's right there," Mike's pal said. "Just introduce me and I'll take it from there."

"Not going to happen," Mike said. "If he speaks or invites us over, I'll introduce you then."

A few minutes later, as Mike and his buddy were coming out of the locker room, Mr. Hogan was standing outside the golf shop chatting with a young couple. "Come on, Mike," his friend said, "he's talking to those people who don't know anything about golf. You don't think he'd rather talk to me?"

Mike chuckled and brought his friend over for an intoduction. They chatted for a few minutes, and Mr. Hogan was his usual polite self. As intimidating as his presence could sometimes seem, once he engaged you, he was genuine and gracious.

Lots of people had similar stories. Robert Stennett, a

member at Shady Oaks who designed fighter jets for Lockheed Martin, brought the pilots from the Air Force Thunderbird exhibition team out for a round of golf. When they went into the grillroom, the pilots wanted Robert to introduce them to Mr. Hogan. At first Robert turned the request down. Then one of the colonels said, "No, seriously, we really would like to meet him." Robert swallowed the lump in his throat and walked over to Mr. Hogan's table.

"Mr. Hogan, I hate to disturb you," he said, "but I have the Air Force Thunderbird pilots out today as guests, and they were wondering if they could meet you."

Mr. Hogan put down his fork, wiped his mouth, and said, "I would be honored."

He spent an hour with the pilots, and would have kept them entertained the rest of the day if they hadn't had to leave for an afternoon meeting. Before they went, he shook every hand and thanked each man for his service. Then he posed for pictures and told them how honored he was to have met them. Despite Robert's initial reservations, it turned out to be a special afternoon for everyone involved. Robert would retire from Lockheed Martin and went on to serve as the executive director of the Ben Hogan Foundation.

I only used Mr. Hogan's intimidating aura to my advantage one time, an innocent incident where he played along perfectly. Mike and I had some friends come from out of town, primarily to play some money games. Oil, cattlemen, and gambling are as ubiquitous as the wind at Shady Oaks. It was nothing for someone to lose a grand or more in some of the bigger games. Mike loves to gamble more than I do. We were competitive but never against each other, so we always wanted to be partners. On this day we had gotten in over our heads. I always entered a match with an idea in mind of how much money I could afford to lose. Through nine holes on this day, we were down twice that amount.

"Why don't you go see if Mr. Hogan wants to come out and watch us?" Mike said.

I knew what he was implying, and under any other circumstances I would have resisted the temptation to use Mr. Hogan to game an opponent, but hey, we were seriously in the hole, and I was sure they would enjoy meeting him. So, at the turn I went into the clubhouse, got a Coke, and waved to him. He stepped outside and I said, "Hey, Mr. Hogan, why don't you come out on the back nine and watch us? It's a nice day, and we're having a little match. You should come out."

He didn't commit, and when I didn't see him as we played the 10th, I figured the plan hadn't worked. Then on the 11th green I saw him. He came up in a golf cart and sat silently behind the green. Our opponents' demeanor changed immediately. Their breathing shallowed and their swings quickened. We introduced our friends and their eyes grew wide.

Mr. Hogan watched us play the 12th hole and he watched us tee off on 13 before heading in. I'm sure he knew what I was doing, and he probably thought it was funny. Our opponents were never the same. The match turned in our favor, and we went from being down more money than I could afford to lose to winning enough for Mike and me to buy dinner.

I always thought of Mr. Hogan as someone I could turn to if I was ever in a tough spot. He was my first phone call when I got my clubs stolen after the last tournament of my first year on tour. It may not sound like a big problem to have your clubs stolen after the last tournament, but I was heading back to tour school in five days. The second phone call I made was to the TaylorMade rep. The one club in my bag that wasn't a Hogan club was my driver. Mr. Hogan hated it with its gold graphite shaft, and never shied away from telling me. He replaced my irons and fairway woods within a day and even sent a few drivers with them, but I could never hit his drivers as well as I could the TaylorMade.

By the next day, all my clubs were replaced except for my wedges. They took a little more time because they were specially ground to be just like Mr. Hogan's, one with more bounce for soft sand and the other with a sharper leading edge for firm sand. Mr. Hogan told me he would bring them out when he came to the course. He showed up early that day. I was hitting balls while Eric filmed my swing with a video camera. Twenty balls or so into the session a golf cart came bouncing up the fairway toward me. Mr. Hogan was at the wheel. He whipped the cart onto the tee, almost running over the camera. Then he hopped out and starting watching. Usually he would have lunch and then come out for an hour or two. That day he must have skipped lunch.

"The wedges weren't ready when I left. Gene will bring them out when they're done." He was referring to Gene Sheeley, his chief club maker.

"I'm sure he has nothing better to do," I said. "Is he upset with me?"

"No, he's delighted to do it. He's a nice man."

"I know he is," I said. "But he's probably not real happy about bringing my wedges all the way out here."

"He doesn't mind. That's his job, to make people happy. And he's an expert. He's one in a million. If we lost him, we would be in a helluva jam. He makes all the models and they're exactly right. He's the best."

We practiced for a while. I wanted to hit my new driver, but I knew how badly he wanted me to scrap that Taylor-Made and play a Hogan driver. I just hated taking it out of the bag. Plus, I knew he would have something to say about it. I figured I would wait him out, but after a while I realized he wasn't going to leave. Two hours into the session, I gave up and grabbed the driver.

"What kind of club is that?" he asked

I knew it was coming. "Uh, this is a TaylorMade," I said.

"A what?"

"A TaylorMade," I said again, without looking up, as I set up for another shot.

"I thought you lost it."

"Yeah, they sent me another one." I kept hitting, trying to move past the subject. Now I knew how Tom had felt when Mr. Hogan asked him if he owned a bicycle.

"They did, did they?" he said. Then he waited a few beats before adding, "Maybe you could get Mr. Taylor to send you a few wedges."

I burst out laughing and walked over to punch him in the arm. "I carry thirteen Hogan clubs and one TaylorMade and you get upset with me."

"I'm not upset," he said, the smile never leaving his face. He pointed to the driver. "Let's see that buggy whip." That was what he called any club with a graphite shaft.

When Clarence Stennett, one of the members at Shady Oaks, got a new custom set of Japanese clubs as a gift from his business partner, he couldn't wait to go and play with them. This was a time when custom-fitted clubs were on the extreme luxury end of the golf spectrum, and they also had graphite shafts. The set must have cost three times the retail amount of a standard set from the golf shop. As Mr. Hogan was walking into the shop that day, he stopped at the golf cart and looked at the clubs.

"What have you got there, Clarence?" he asked.

"Oh, it's a custom-made set of clubs my partner gave me as a gift."

Mr. Hogan studied the clubs for a second. "He didn't do you any favors." With that, he turned and retreated to his table.

Unfortunately, one of the wedges Mr. Hogan had custom-made for me didn't work out, and I was running out of time.

"Just take mine," he said. "It's exactly like the one that got stolen."

And that's how I ended up going through LPGA Qualifying School with Ben Hogan's sand wedge in my bag.

There were times when I would try to get him to come out, if for nothing more than for a little exercise. I tried on one especially hot afternoon, when he hadn't practiced in a while, but my plan backfired. "Why don't you come out?"

"No, it's too hot," he said.

"Oh, it's not too bad," I said. "Just come out for a little while."

He pointed to the large windows overlooking the 18th fairway. "Just go outside there and hit some down the fairway."

"I don't think that's such a—"

"Do you want help or not?"

"Yes, I do, but—"

"Then go out and hit it down that fairway."

I did as I was told, and he watched me through the window of the men's grill. There weren't a lot of people playing. It was really hot, but as expected, the first group that came down the 18th fairway had a conniption fit when they saw me. It was a member and three guests and I'm sure they were wondering what the heck was going on. I was trying to apologize and explain at the same time as they marched up to the clubhouse ready to complain. Then they saw Mr. Hogan standing in the window watching me. There was no further discussion, and nobody else complained.

That was so typical. The unapproachable attitude was always there, the demeanor that said, "I dare you to confront me." He used it to get what he wanted at times, and also to keep people at a distance.

During one of my many putting slumps, I was in search of a different putter, and he said, "Let me see what I've got."

He came out to the putting green with some of the ugliest putters I'd ever seen. I actually laughed when he handed one to me. "I can't putt with that," I said. "It's terrible looking."

"Yeah. It only won sixty-four touraments. I don't know how you could make anything with it." He loved sarcasm.

Later, when I was telling my parents the story, my dad said, "Kris, you cannot insult Ben Hogan's putter."

"Don't worry, Dad," I said. "He knows it's ugly."

My good friend Bob Wynn recently told me that Mr. Hogan said I would never make it on tour because I wasn't a good enough putter. Of course, he never told me that. Although we worked little on putting together, he continually searched for a putter that would help my game.

Giving was important to him, but it was done in private and never talked about. The generosity that he showed Valerie's sister, Sarah Harriman, and her family was a prime example. Sarah lived just a few houses down from Mr. and Mrs. Hogan and the families were inseparable when I knew them. The Hogans had Sarah and her daughter and granddaughter over for dinner at least two or three times a week, and Mr. Hogan made sure they all had whatever they needed.

When Sarah's granddaughter, Lisa Scott, was in high school, Mr. Hogan pulled her aside and said, "Do you make good grades?"

"Yes, Uncle Ben," Lisa said.

"Good. I don't want you to worry about college. If you keep your grades up, all your college expenses will be taken care of."

Not only did he pay for Lisa's education, he gave her a monthly stipend while she was in school, and would occasionally slip her a hundred dollars on the side. "It was more money than I'd ever had in my life," she told me later. "One time he knocked on the door of my grandmother's house and when I stepped out he handed me two hundred and fifty dollars.

When I said, 'Uncle Ben, I don't need this money. You're already paying for school and giving me money every month.' He said, 'You keep that. It'll be our secret.'" It was his secret, one of the many he intentionally kept from the world.

The idea of putting on a mask for the public is nothing new. Celebrities have been doing it for as long as there have been fans. The character Mr. Hogan created helped perpetuate the mystique that still surrounds him today. But the real Mr. Hogan was the man who cut his banana in half for me every Monday, the man who would toss me a Snickers bar as he rode past in his cart, the man who would press his nose against the window to make faces at small children, and the man who generously and quietly gave to those whom he saw were in need.

One day Mr. Hogan and I were out testing drivers. One of his biggest frustrations was that I could never get a Hogan driver in my bag. He decided that a little lead tape would help one of the drivers we were working with. We went into the pro-shop, and he was grumbling and stomping around, in a real snit. The head pro and his assistant couldn't find the lead tape and that was making him even angrier. While they were looking, a man came into the shop with his young son on his shoulder. The second Mr. Hogan saw the child, his whole demeanor changed. His face lit up and he softened immediately. He walked right up to the child, without looking at his father, and pinched his cheek.

"Weelll, who do we have here?" he said. He spent the next couple of minutes making motorboat noises to the delight of the child, and even more so, the father. He was saying things like, "Are you going to be a golfer when you get older?" He went on and on. As soon as they left, he went back in the bag room stomping and grumbling about the lead tape. I remember the three of us just looking at one another in amazement.

Just like that, the mask had fallen away, and everyone within earshot got a glimpse of the real person. A glimpse of the Mr. Hogan I knew.

"LET'S PLAY THE BACK NINE."

✦

It's easy to celebrate the "firsts" in life, First Communion, the first win, birth of a first child. These are all events that can be enjoyed instantly because of their primacy. Everyone recognizes when something happens for the first time. The same cannot be said for our "lasts." It is only through the prism of hindsight that we know we've seen something special for the last time. Anybody can tell you that Neil Armstrong was the first man to walk on the moon, for example, but very few remember that Gene Cernan was the last, because we didn't know at the time that we wouldn't be going back. No one in the ballpark knew that Hank Aaron's 755th home run would be his last, and those who thought they had seen Brett Favre play his final game in Green Bay in 2007 soon realized that you never know how or when the "lasts" in life will happen.

So on Wednesday, August 27, 1986, when Mr. Hogan finally agreed to my repeated requests to play an actual round, neither of us knew that it would be the last round of golf he would ever play. I guess I always thought he would come out and join me again, even though he'd consistently turned me down up until that point. We would play a few holes here and there but never a complete round. One afternoon, Tom Byrum and I were playing when he rode out to watch us. He played the final four holes on the back nine with us that day, using Tom's clubs (referring to them as buggy whips the whole time). He shot one-under in that abbreviated round with one birdie and three pars, but he'd never played a whole round with me.

I certainly didn't understand the historical significance of what was going to happen that warm August Thursday. As part of our usual banter, I would say things like "Hey, we've got a match tomorrow, why don't you come out and play with us?" And he would say, "No, maybe another time." That was no great surprise. Given the obvious pain in his legs and hips, I was fortunate that he still knocked a few balls around on the Little Nine. So I was shocked when, on this day, he responded to my usual "Why don't we play tomorrow?" with a "That would be fine."

My surprise must have been apparent. He almost laughed as he said, "Around one o'clock?"

"Sure," I said. Then I decided to push my luck. "Should I invite a couple of my teammates?"

When he said yes I almost fainted. The team didn't play Shady Oaks on Thursdays, but the pro occasionally let me bring a group out. Because we were broke college kids he wouldn't charge them guest fees, which was the only way any of them would have come. This time, I invited my roommate Kirsten Larson. She is the type of person who never has a bad day and if she does, you would never know it. Mr. Hogan knew and liked her. She was one of the select few whom Mr. Hogan didn't mind having along for our Little Nine practice sessions. The other player I invited was Ellie Gibson, one of the best players on our team. Mr. Hogan had watched her hit balls a few times and I knew she would be pretty comfortable with him. (Well, as comfortable as you can be playing nine holes with Ben Hogan.)

I wasn't 100 percent sure he was going to show up—not that he was prone to reneging on commitments, but if he woke up sore or stiff it would have been easy and understandable for him to beg off, so I didn't tell my teammates who our fourth would be for that day. The following afternoon, Thursday, August 28, 1986, Ellie, Kirsten, and I slung our bags on our shoulders and headed to the range.

I hadn't seen Mr. Hogan yet that day. I would have put the odds at about fifty-fifty that he would make it. I think he enjoyed spending time with me, but he wasn't comfortable being on display, especially swinging a golf club. People had certain expectations of him and he felt it was not enough to go out and bunt a few shots down the fairway.

When Shoal Creek Golf Club opened in Birmingham, Alabama, in 1977, Hal Thompson, the heavy-equipment dealer who owned the club, asked four former U.S. Open champions to play the inaugural round. Jack Nicklaus was in, because he had designed Shoal Creek, and Jerry Pate and Hubert Green agreed because they were natives of Alabama. Mr. Hogan was asked to round out the foursome. It took him two weeks to make his decision. He got back into practice mode and seriously considered it. In the end, though, he didn't feel like his game was good enough to be exhibited. He thanked Mr. Thompson and said, "I know you don't mind if I don't play well, and maybe the spectators wouldn't care. But I care."

I understood how he felt, so I was pleasantly surprised when he drove up right on time and asked if we were ready. I walked over to his cart and told him I was glad he'd made it.

"I'm glad I made it too," he laughed. "Let's play the back nine."

And with that he drove to the blue tees of the 10th hole.

I turned around to face my still shocked teammates. "We're playing with Mr. Hogan?" Ellie asked.

"No way!" Kirsten said, more to herself than to either of us.

"Yep," I answered. "He's our fourth."

If anybody had known this was going to be Mr. Hogan's final round, there certainly would have been more fanfare. Instead, we simply walked to the tee. My teammates, still in shock, stood motionless with their mouths open while Mr. Hogan teed up a ball, took a couple of abbreviated practice swings, and promptly duck-hooked his first shot of the day past a line of oaks separating the 10th fairway from the driving range.

I had very rarely seen him hit a shot that bad. I wasn't sure if he would tee up another or go hit it from the range. Driving the ball well was always a source of pride with him. He thought the driver was the most important club in the bag. "The tee shot sets up how you play the hole," he always said. He also believed that it was important to be able to curve shots with the driver both right and left at will. "Hitting a straight ball is an accident," he said often. Today that's not the case, but when Mr. Hogan played, the greatest compliment a player could receive was that he "worked the ball" well, which is harder to do with today's equipment. He got in his cart and watched us hit our drives. He was seventy-five years old and hadn't hit a single warm-up ball. I guess we all thought he should never miss a fairway, but since that wasn't reality even when he was winning championships, it was unrealistic to expect it in a casual round with us.

The 10th is an uphill par-4 that measures 425 yards from

the back tees where Mr. Hogan hit, but it plays longer than that because of the hill and the prevailing headwind. Throw in the fact that the trees on both sides of the fairway give you a narrow tunnel, it's a tough way to open the back nine, and a very hard hole to start your round.

My teammates and I played from the white tees, several yards ahead of Mr. Hogan. From the tips, Shady Oaks is a little longer than 7,000 yards. Kirsten, Ellie, and I played from the tees that measured about 6,300 yards, the average length of a course on the LPGA Tour at the time. No one would have begrudged Mr. Hogan playing from a tee that was a little farther up, but he would have none of it. Even at his age, he felt as though, as a male professional, he should play the course from the back tees. From back there it was a lot of golf course no matter how well you hit it.

As my teammates and I walked down the fairway, Mr. Hogan drove his cart silently through the left rough. By the time we got to our shots, he had already taken a low iron and punched the ball out of the trees and onto the fairway. From there, he hit what appeared to be a solid middle iron that flew just long and a little right of the green. I immediately felt bad for having asked him to come out. It looked like he was going to make double bogey or worse on his 1st hole. The pin was cut near the front right and he was in the high grass with twenty feet of green between his ball and the hole. It was a straight downhill shot. Not the leave he wanted, I was sure.

He got to his ball and pulled out what looked like his Equalizer—the Hogan Company name for their pitching wedge. Then he hit what we all thought was a scull. The ball shot out of the rough and never got above waist height. I don't know if I said, "Get down!" out loud or just thought it, but I was sure he had bladed his fourth shot over the green and would be heading down the fairway for his next shot, wondering why the hell he'd decided to join us. What we saw next seemed impossible. The ball took one hop and stopped about a foot from the hole. It was like this low, screaming shot hit flypaper. I couldn't believe my eyes. I looked at Ellie and Kirsten and they had the same incredulous look on their faces that I'm sure I had on mine. I think I managed to say, "Nice shot!"

He just calmly walked up and tapped in his putt for bogey.

As we were walking to the next hole, Ellie said, "Could you believe that shot?"

"I couldn't believe my eyes," I said.

Then Kirsten piped in with "I thought I might have him on that hole."

We laughed. She couldn't be serious about wanting to beat him, could she?

He hit first throughout the round because his tees were behind ours. I don't think he went full-out on many drives. He could hit it long when he wanted to and he only wanted to on a couple holes that day. Most people don't realize how long Mr. Hogan once hit the ball. Before Augusta National built their little course and started the annual Wednesday Par Three Contest, they held a long-drive competition the day before the Masters. Mr. Hogan won it several times, a fact that had to drive the other players nuts, especially those who were six or seven inches taller and a hundred pounds heavier than he. At seventy-five, he could still belt it past all of us girls if he put a little *oomph* into it. Since he was hitting first from tees that were ten to fifty yards behind ours, Ellie and I were able to hit our tee shots beyond Mr. Hogan's for most of the round. Kirsten was a shorter hitter, so her best pokes were about even with his drives. That certainly made hiding her Ping golf clubs from him a lot tougher, but that didn't stop her from trying. Every hole, we noticed Kirsten draping her towel over her irons in the impossible hope that Mr. Hogan wouldn't notice that she wasn't playing Hogan clubs. The funny part was, she had played with Hogan clubs her whole life, and had only recently changed to Pings. Ellie and I chuckled about it for most of the afternoon.

On 11, another 425-yard par-4 with a fairway that swooped down from the tee and then back up toward the green, Mr. Hogan hit a perfect drive in the middle of the fairway. My ball was fifteen to twenty yards ahead, so I waited to watch him hit his approach. He didn't take much time. The pin was cut center-right. That is a tricky pin placement because the green looks big but doesn't play big. It's like a lot of the shots on links courses in Great Britain and Ireland, in that it looks from the fairway or tee like you have a lot of room. But when you get there you find out your landing area is much smaller than you realized. On the 11th hole at Shady Oaks, if you hit your approach long or a little right, it funnels off the green, leaving you with a difficult twenty-yard pitch. Mr. Hogan knew all of that, and he hit a great shot with a 5-wood. The ball stopped exactly pin-high, ten feet left of the hole. It was the perfect leave.

Kirsten looked at me and rolled her eyes. Neither of us could believe what a great shot he had just hit, and I couldn't believe the kind of reaction Kirsten had to it. She was serious about beating him. Five minutes later, Mr. Hogan rolled his ten-foot birdie putt into the center of the hole. Two holes into the round, he was even par, and two strokes ahead of Kirsten in a match he had no idea he was playing.

I'm not sure how many clubs he carried, but he had to have been violating the fourteen-club rule. That wasn't unusual. He normally carried a strong 4-wood and a 5-wood, along with an assortment of long irons and wedges. This was before the days of titanium drivers and hybrids of every shape, size, and degree, but Mr. Hogan was still a tinkerer. He always had an extra wood or a new model iron in his bag. Those who thought he was a strict conformist never saw the assortment of prototypes lying around in the bag room at Shady Oaks. Mr. Hogan dabbled with metal woods and hybrids long before they were in vogue, and he had wedges with sixty-five degrees of loft decades before most manufacturers discovered them.

At the 12th, I thought he might hit his 5-wood or maybe even his strong 4-wood. The par-3 played almost 240 yards from the tips. A good portion of the Shady Oak membership couldn't reach that green with their best shots, but Mr. Hogan had played it often enough to know what he was doing.

Anyone who had ever played with him had a story, and one of the founding members, Tex Moncrief, loved recounting a round in which he made a side bet with Mr. Hogan at the 12th: "Ben, you want to play up and down for fifty dollars?" Tex had asked. This was a closest-to-the-pin game with the added twist that if the person who lost the closest-to-the-pin won the hole, the bet flipped. So, if you hit your shot ten feet from the hole and were closest, but your opponent hit it fifteen feet and made the putt, you either had to make your putt or lose the bet. According to Tex, Mr. Hogan stared at him for a second and said, "I'll play you for fifty thousand if you want." To which Tex replied, "No, I just want a friendly game," so they settled on the fifty-dollar bet. Tex hit it close on 12 and won, but when they got to the second par-3 on the back 9, the 16th, Mr. Hogan's demeanor changed. The laser focus of his championship days returned, if only for a moment, and he hit his shot to five feet and made his birdie to win back the fifty dollars he'd lost at 12.

Nothing was on the line this time (at least not for him).

He hit his ball pin-high twenty feet right of the hole, calmly two-putted for par and headed to the next tee.

Thirteen was another healthy par-4, coming in at just under 440 yards from the tips. It required a long, well-positioned tee shot, which Mr. Hogan easily hit. It was the one time when I felt like he went after his drive to get the most out of it. As a result, he was on the left side of the fairway a little farther than Ellie and me, and well ahead of where Kirsten hit her tee shot. As we were standing in the left rough waiting for Kirsten to play, Mr. Hogan pulled up beside me and said in a low voice, "Do you think Kurshin would be offended if I gave her my heavy club to swing for a couple of weeks?" He always called her Kurshin. I'm not sure why but Kurshin and I had plenty of laughs over it.

I find it so interesting that Mr. Hogan would worry about offending a young college girl by giving her some help. Most people would have paid any amount of money for advice from him. He wanted to give Kirsten one of his homemade (and ahead-of-its-time) training aids to help increase her distance off the tee. Long before swing fans or the Medicus heavy golf clubs, Mr. Hogan drilled some holes in the head of a persimmon driver and filled them with lead. The club weighed probably five pounds, and swinging it more than once or twice would get your heart rate up. He used it as an exercise tool well into his seventies, and he believed, rightly so, that five or ten minutes a day with a weighted club would increase your strength and clubhead speed through impact. With Kirsten hitting her best drives twenty to thirty yards behind the rest of us, Mr. Hogan thought she could use the help but was sensitive enough to worry about hurting her feelings. I told him I felt sure she wouldn't be offended if he gave her the weighted club for a few weeks.

Kirsten had no idea we were having this discussion at the time. She was too busy grinding out her approach at 13 in the hopes of getting back to even with Mr. Hogan. She hit a great shot to just below the hole, leaving herself a birdie opportunity. The pin was cut on the left of the right-to-left sloping green, so that any shot right of the flag left you with a downhill putt. Mr. Hogan hit a pure 5-iron shot that started just right of the flag and faded toward the center of the green. That left him with a downhill eighteen-foot putt that he hit way too hard.

His putting stroke always looked a little short and quick to me, like a boxer popping his opponent with a short, quick jab. I'm sure that stroke was born of old putting surfaces. Looking back at some of the old tournament films from Mr. Hogan's era, the greens appeared bumpy and slow. Even Masters footage from the forties and fifties shows players rapping putts so hard that they would run off any modern green. Players who came up in that time developed firm, popping putting strokes that allowed them to hit the ball hard without the ball losing its line. Mr. Hogan never made the change to the slower, more flowing putting stroke required for modern, faster greens. Couple that with the loss of touch that comes with age and the loss of depth perception from near total blindness in one eye, and it was easy to understand why his putting went south.

I wasn't surprised when he missed the six-footer coming back up the hill at 13 and made bogey. Kirsten missed her birdie putt and didn't look happy, but she did march to the 14th tee with a renewed sense of purpose. He was one over par through four holes. In her mind, she still had a chance to beat him.

Holes 14 and 15 at Shady Oaks are the lowest points on the golf course, back-to-back parallel par-5s with a creek that comes into play on both holes. Fourteen can be a risk/reward hole. If you can bomb a tee shot and hug the creek line, you have a chance of getting an equally well-struck second shot onto the green. The safer play, and the approach I always took to the hole, was to hit a good drive down the left-center of the fairway and then lay up short and left of the green with a middle to a long iron. That left you with a straightforward wedge shot into a small green that you couldn't afford to miss. Anything long, whether left or right of the green, made for a difficult par.

Mr. Hogan played it the way the architect intended. He hit a good drive down the left side of the fairway and a perfect layup with a middle iron. From there he chose not to attack the flag, which was tucked on the front left portion of the green. He hit it to the middle of the green, leaving himself a twelve-footer for birdie.

There is a great story about how he once prepped the battlefield to his advantage. One of the standard big-money games at Shady Oaks is something called "the swing." In it, one twosome takes on every combination of every other group in the game. So, if there are twelve players, the group that has the swing has forty-five bets, a bet with every combination of twosome among the other ten players. If the bet is a $10 nassau (front, back, and overall), the swing group has $1,350 on the line. It could get so confusing that figuring out the bet might take up to an hour after the round, but the swing group always stood to win or lose a lot of money. (I know this is confusing. I had to go to my brother for this information and I'm still not sure I understand it!) One day Mr. Hogan and Earl Baldridge had the swing and lost big. They went into the men's grill and paid up, but Mr. Hogan was not happy. He asked if they could have the swing the next day and everyone was happy to oblige. Mr. Hogan went out on the course with the superintendent that afternoon and picked every tee and pin placement, setting the course up for exactly the kinds of shots he wanted to play. It only took a few holes the next day for everyone to realize he had gotten them. There was a lot of grumbling that afternoon when he set his hat in the middle of the table to collect his money, but every person left with another legendary Hogan story.

He had nothing to do with the course setup the day we played. If he had, I'm certain he wouldn't have tucked the pin front-left on 14. He hit a good putt, but his twelve-footer slid below the hole, and he tapped in for a routine par.

I matched him shot for shot on 14, and I also bummed some rides. (When Kirsten, Ellie, and I got together to re-count these nine holes, they both informed me I rode most of the time. Just for the record, I'm sure they are exaggerating.) I do know Mr. Hogan and I chatted about whatever popped into our heads. I was just so happy that he was out playing again. I'm not sure how long it had been since he had actually played a round. We would go out for a few holes after practic-ing on the Little Nine every now and then, but that was just practice. Other than the holes he had played with Tom and me, I'd never seen him playing an actual round, and I had no idea when he'd done it last.

By the time we got to the 15th tee that afternoon, it felt to me like any other day at Shady Oaks. That was what made Kirsten's internal blood-match so funny. She played each shot like it was the final round of a major, while Mr. Hogan was making comments like "Don't you ever polish your shoes?" when I put my feet on the dash of the cart.

Mr. Hogan looked very comfortable on the tee at 15. He hit a perfect shot that fell a little left and ran out in front of the creek. A lot of people assumed that he only faded the ball after he changed his grip and beat the hooks. But that was never the case. He always told me that you should hit the shot that each hole requires. He worked the ball left and right, flying it high and low, depending on what was needed. Fifteen at Shady Oaks required a draw off the tee in order to get it closer to the green for your second shot, and that was exactly the shot he hit.

Unfortunately, Kirsten's goal of beating Mr. Hogan hit a rough patch at 15, when she hit it in the trees on the right side of the fairway. She banged around in the rough and trees while Mr. Hogan hit a great second shot to within sixty yards of the hole. Ellie and I weren't paying much attention to our games at that time, but we both hit that green in regulation and missed our birdie putts. Mr. Hogan hit another low, driving wedge shot that looked initially like it had been caught thin. When it hit, the ball took one hop forward, spun slightly to the left, and stopped dead six feet below the hole. He hit a perfect putt that went in for birdie.

He always talked to me about "leaves," not leaves on a tree, but where you wanted to leave a shot relative to the pin. The approach shot that he hit on 15 was a perfect example of that. Given where the pin was cut, any ball hit short and slightly left of the hole would leave a straight uphill putt. That was where Mr. Hogan hit his wedge shot. If he'd hit it three feet from the hole, but long and right, the shot would not have been as good even though the ball would have been closer to the hole. It wasn't enough to know where the pin was cut: He believed you also had to know the fall line of a green, so that you always knew where to leave the ball to give yourself the easiest possible putt. He said he never aimed directly at pins because he was afraid he'd hit them. "A good shot can turn into a bad shot real fast."

That wasn't much of an issue on the par-3 16th. The green on this 155-yard hole is very shallow, with trouble lurking in front and behind. It's critical that you hit it the right distance. Mr. Hogan hit the ball just a fraction long, leaving himself with a twenty-five-footer from the back fringe on a green that ran away from him. This was one of those situations where the risk of trying to leave the ball below the hole was not worth the potential reward. With almost no green below the hole, there was no way he was going to risk flying his shot pin high with a 6-iron.

All the rest of us found the green and two-putted for pars. Mr. Hogan made another stabbing stroke with his long putt, and the ball ran five feet past. He missed the five-footer coming back for his second 3-putt bogey of the round.

Through 16 he was one-over par. Kirsten would later tell me that when he missed that putt she remembered thinking she still had a chance, however slim. She had fallen three shots behind him after botching the 15th, but her par on 16 put her only two shots back with two difficult finishing holes to play.

Seventeen was a tough hole under the best of circumstances. It was 390 uphill yards, with a progressively narrowing fairway. Because of the severity of the slope, you had to hit a good tee shot to get to the 150-yard marker, which sat atop a slight plateau. But if you pulled your drive a little left, you could be blocked out by trees, with the ball well below your feet. Miss it right and you had tree trouble as well. Any shot off line was an almost certain bogey.

Mr. Hogan hit a good tee shot down the middle, but it didn't get to the plateau. The ball hit into the hill and got no roll at all, leaving him a lengthy approach. Kirsten hit a solid drive that rolled about a foot past Mr. Hogan's ball, and Ellie and I hit our balls to the 150-yard marker.

The hole was so steep from where Mr. Hogan was that he couldn't see the putting surface from the fairway, and Mr. Hogan's eyesight was so bad, he couldn't find the pin against the backdrop of trees and blue sky. "Kurshin, where's the flag?" he asked Kirsten.

"It's about ten yards right of the front-left bunker, Mr. Hogan," she said. That was the middle of the green.

He nodded and drew the 5-wood out of his bag. Uphill and into a healthy breeze, this was probably the toughest approach shot he'd had all day. I didn't give him much of a chance of getting it close. He'd struck the ball beautifully after the 1st hole, but there was only so much you could expect.

What followed next was a shot we all recalled as one of the best we'd ever seen. Even though he was hitting a shot from an uphill lie, he made a balanced swing and the ball shot off the face like it had been fired from a gun. It started at the edge of the bunker and faded right at the flag, a shot all of us knew was going to be close before it landed. From how it looked when it came down on top of the flag, I wouldn't have been surprised if it had gone in the hole. When we got to the green, we saw that he'd hit it within five feet of the hole, a putt he made easily for another birdie.

Even though Kirsten knew her quest to beat him was over at that point, she couldn't stop praising the 5-wood shot. It was a great birdie on a tough hole, and one of the finest approaches any of us had ever seen.

I know people have said that he could go an entire round without saying a word, but that was not the case with us. As we played he complimented us when we hit good shots, and by the time we had played a few holes he had made us all feel comfortable enough to relax and chat easily.

On the 18th hole, he did not hit a great drive. The ball flew straight, and most people would have been thrilled to have it. But given how well he'd hit it up until that point, it was obvious that this wasn't his most solid strike. As a result he was left with a long approach into the 430-yard final hole and he had to hit another wood. This was a hole that he'd once been able to play with a driver and a short iron, but he didn't complain about his lack of distance or the need to hit woods for so many of his approaches. He just retooled his strategy and played the shot that was required each time.

His final approach was another solid shot that looked great leaving the clubface. The ball flew right over the flag and landed about twenty feet past the hole. One hop and it was in a difficult back bunker. Giving him the fringe on 16, it was his first missed green since the 10th, and his only bunker shot of the day. It was no easy one either. The pin was front-middle, which meant it was a touchy bunker shot with a green that sloped hard away from him. It was almost impossible to get close.

It would have been easy to get upset. He had hit a great shot that ended up in the bunker, but he didn't seem bothered. As he had with every other shot in the round, he checked his grip, stepped into his setup, waggled, and swung without a moment's hesitation. The ball popped out onto the putting surface and ran right down to the hole. But then it kept rolling. There was no way to stop it on the fast downslope that was the 18th green, so it rolled fifteen feet beyond the pin. He showed no emotion as he lined up the putt, but the stroke looked a little smoother than some of his other efforts. When the ball hit the center of the cup and fell in for a par, he said, "If I'd putted like this, I might not have quit playing."

The two 3-putt bogeys were forgotten, as was the twelve-foot birdie putt on 14 that never stood a chance of going in. He'd finished with a five-foot birdie putt on 17 and a fifteen-foot par-save on 18, and in his mind he'd putted great.

He'd shot even par for nine holes, which was a great feat for a man of any age on a course as tough as Shady Oaks. The fact that he was in his mid-seventies and hadn't played a round of golf in years made it even more amazing. It was an impressive feat, but there certainly weren't any fireworks going off when we finished.

Eleven years earlier, Mr. Hogan had gone out for another casual round with Bill Flynn, John Miles, and Joe Cates. He shot a course-record 64 at Shady Oaks, which also happened to be his age at the time. That sparked quite the celebration. *Golf Digest* printed a story about it, and I think it meant quite a bit to Mr. Hogan because after the round, sitting at his table, he'd said, "Bill, would you go get the scorecard? I'd like to keep it." Bill hadn't kept the card, so he went looking for Joe to get it.

When he found Joe at the card table playing gin, he said, "Hey, Joe, the Hawk wants the card."

Joe didn't even look up from his gin hand as he said, "Nope. I kept score and I'm keeping the card."

Bill gulped and delivered the news back to Mr. Hogan, who nodded without getting upset and said, "I understand. Bill, just go get three more scorecards and fill them out. We'll all sign them and that way each of us can have a card."

Everyone in the group got a card, but Joe Cates got the original. It was the talk of the town for days. But, then again, it was a first. Mr. Hogan had never shot his age, and no one had ever shot 64 at Shady Oaks before that day.

It's impossible to know if he would have broken his age if he'd played the front nine with Kirsten, Ellie, and me, but I wouldn't have bet against it. After the round, he asked us if we wanted to go into the mixed grill and have a drink. Since none of us knew this would be the last nine holes he would ever play, our celebration consisted of Diet Dr Pepper for us and a vodka martini with extra olives for him, which hopefully helped the obvious pain in his knee. We chatted while we drank. I told him it was a great bunker shot he'd hit on the 18th, even though it didn't turn out well. He said, "Johnny Revolta would have made it. I was more nervous when Johnny hit it in a bunker than when he hit the green. He was liable to make it from the bunker." We all laughed.

He encouraged each of us and complimented us on our games. He told us about how he had started playing left-handed because the first club given to him was left-handed. When he finally got right-handed clubs he played cross-handed for a while and then settled into a conventional grip. When it was time to leave I stopped at the bar to talk to Sandy the bartender. Mr. Hogan came up and thanked me again for the game. Imagine that. He was thanking me! I noticed he had his foot on the brass footrail around the bar. It made me smile recalling how much he hated it when they put it in. He had said to me at that time, "Don't you think it looks awful?" I thought it looked fine and told him so.

"It looks terrible! It looks like it should be in a brothel." I laughed and went on my way.

Then I left for a tournament and was gone for about five days. When I came back to the club, several people told me Mr. Hogan had been looking for me. I thought, *Uh-oh. What have I done?* When I saw him, he started apologizing for having used such coarse language in front of a young lady. I had no idea what he was talking about. Then I realized that he was referring to using the word *brothel* in our conversation. I had to laugh; I didn't mention that I had recently seen *The Best Little Whorehouse in Texas*!

I could never look at that railing again without smiling.

I thanked him again for joining me and my teammates. Then I went back out to practice and Mr. Hogan went to his table in the men's grill. And just like that, his final round ended with a quiet good-bye.

But years later, Mike Wright, the head pro at Shady Oaks, confirmed what I believed to be true. He had never played another round after that nine-hole afternoon with Ellie, Kirsten, and me.

"I WANTED TO GET MY NAME UP ON THAT WALL."

Our routine continued even though I graduated from TCU in 1987. I played a handful of mini-tour events before going to LPGA Qualifying School in the fall, but throughout that time and for several years after, I stayed in Fort Worth. It was a great town to base myself out of once I joined the LPGA Tour. Texas is basically the middle of the country, so getting to events rarely required more than a two-hour flight, and the Dallas–Fort Worth Airport is one of the most convenient to fly in and out of. You are never more than fifty yards from the curb to your gate, and never more than a hundred feet from your bags when you land. Plus, Eric was at TCU by then, and Mike stayed in town as well. He and I bought houses next to each other and we both continued practicing at Shady Oaks.

Mr. Hogan stayed right where he'd been since the day I met him. He continued to go to his office at the Ben Hogan Company every morning, even though a group of Japanese investors had bought his company and many of their decisions baffled him. For example, in 1989, the new owners chartered a jet to fly a sushi chef from Tokyo to Augusta to prepare blow-fish for eight people during the Masters. Like clockwork, he left the office around 11:40 and drove twenty minutes to Shady Oaks, following the same route at the same speed. One day my brother Eric, running late as usual, got stuck behind him. Eric tailgated and swore for several miles until he finally passed the puttering motorist. He was ready to give him a dirty look when he realized it was Mr. Hogan. Eric immediately smiled and waved, but of course Mr. Hogan wasn't paying attention.

Like his golf swing and demeanor, very little in Mr. Hogan's life changed. He parked his Cadillac in the closest spot to the front of the club, came through the lightly stained oak doors, spoke to the receptionist, went to the men's grill, and sat down at his big round table for lunch. When I was in town he would come out to the Little Nine to watch and help, although his own hitting tapered off after 1990. I continued to tell him he should go to the Masters and hit the ceremonial first drive. Everyone would love it and they would be shocked by how well he could still hit it. "No, no," he said. "I'm done traveling. If I were going to travel, I'd go to Seminole and see my good friend George Coleman."

The truth was, even when he was playing he didn't like to travel. His legs ached so much that flying was awful for him. As a young woman in my twenties, I couldn't fully appreciate the kind of pain he must have felt, but since then I've had seven hip surgeries in nine years. Now I can empathize.

Years before, a Japanese company had been in Florida filming an ad that would only air in Japan. Sam Snead, Lee Trevino, and Gene Sarazen were in the ad, but the company wanted Mr. Hogan. The money was incredible, but Mr. Hogan said no. It wasn't worth getting on a plane. Snead even called and said, "Ben, it's one day's work and it's a pot load of money," but Mr. Hogan wasn't going to fly. He finally said, "If they don't mind spending that kind of money, why don't you come here?" And that's exactly what happened. The Japanese company chartered a plane and flew everyone to Fort Worth and Mr. Hogan appeared with them in the ad.

His dislike for travel only added to his reputation as a loner. The members at Winged Foot in Mamaroneck, New York, had a policy of giving a membership to a great player and ambassador of the game. When Bobby Jones died, the members gave his membership to Mr. Hogan. Unfortunately, he never used it. Not once. Doing so would have required a trip to New York, a trip he was no longer willing to take no matter how nice the perks.

People were shocked when he traveled to Los Angeles in 1987 to film a commercial at Riviera. David Hueber, who was president of the Ben Hogan Company at the time, had to plead with him for months to get him to star in ads for his own company. "Mr. Hogan, we really need you to help us with this new product launch," Hueber said. When Mr. Hogan finally agreed, Hueber said, "Great, I'll set something up at Riviera," to which Mr. Hogan replied, "Why can't we film it here?"

He wasn't really a recluse. He preferred being around people who knew him so he wouldn't have to engage in small talk. When he met someone for the first time, they wanted to talk about golf and he wanted to talk about anything but golf. He complained about having to go on that Riviera trip right up until the day he left, and when he came back, he complained some more. I knew he would never leave Fort Worth again.

Even though I never thought about it at the time, my relationship with Mr. Hogan was kind of a local secret. Everyone at Shady Oaks knew we were friends, but not many people outside of Fort Worth knew. That was fine with me. I never told people that Mr. Hogan was, in essence, my teacher. In fact, I very rarely even mentioned that I knew him. It was pretty easy since his name didn't usually come up in casual conversation. The few times I told someone that I knew him, it almost felt as if I lost my credibility. Consequently, I avoided mentioning his name to anyone other than genuine admirers of his. I remember hitting balls at a tournament one day when a caddy told me he liked my swing. Then he started yammering about all the people he had caddied for, including the time he caddied for Mr. Hogan in the 1954 U.S. Open. I listened politely. I could tell he enjoyed talking, so I didn't interrupt. About twenty minutes into his monologue, someone else walked up and asked me where I practiced in Fort Worth. I said, "Shady Oaks," and I saw a light go on in the caddy's head. The look on his face was worth the lost twenty minutes of practice.

Mr. Hogan continued to help me in any way he could after I turned pro. During my rookie season he knew we were playing in Fort Lauderdale. "Why don't you go over and play Seminole?" he asked. "It's a great course for practice. I'll get you all set up."

I told him I'd let him know if we had time. I don't usually play other courses when I'm playing in a tournament, but when I told my caddy that we had the option of playing Seminole, he said, "Are you crazy? We're playing!"

Caddies don't normally talk to their bosses that way, but this was my first year on tour and my caddy, Gerry Summa, was a friend of the family who was between regular jobs when my dad hired him to go out with me for the year. I didn't know him very well, but he turned out to be one of the funniest people I've ever met. He would say things like "A scared dog can't hunt" while I was deciding if I should go for a risky shot. Then, after I hit it in the water, he'd drop his head and say, "Neither can a dead one."

We bought an old RV to travel in and give Gerry a place to sleep. We called it the Road Warrior, but it could have been called the Rusted Wreck. Imagine all those RVs you see in campgrounds on the sides of the interstate highways in places you wouldn't stop on a bet, and you'll have a mental picture of how we traveled. We were quite the spectacle when we pulled up to the guardhouse at one of America's most exclusive golf clubs in our salt-rusted RV with South Dakota plates.

When we got to the tiny guardhouse, the guard looked at us like we smelled. He offered a contemptuous "Can I help you?" He was getting ready to give us directions back to the highway when I said, "Yes, we're here to play."

"Uh-huh." He was toying with us.

"No, we are," I said.

He almost laughed, but not quite. "And who would be the member sponsoring you today?"

Here it comes, loss of credibility. I paused and said, "Ben Hogan."

This time he did laugh before saying, "Yeah, right!"

Before he could shoo us along, I said, "No, really, Ben Hogan."

He still hadn't looked at his book and I didn't think he was going to, so I said, "It's either under Ben Hogan or George Coleman." I think George Coleman was president of the club at the time. If it was possible, I lost even more credibility with that name.

I tried again. "Will you please just call?"

The guard sighed and made what he thought would be a perfunctory call to the clubhouse. Then his eyes got wide. He came back and said, "I'm so sorry, Ms. Tschetter. Welcome to Seminole. Just pull up front. They'll take care of your, er, vehicle and get you set up with a locker." We had a great time that day and the people at Seminole couldn't have been nicer.

On tour I never talked about who was teaching me. Imagine the eye-rolling reactions I would have gotten if I'd said, "Oh, yeah, when I'm home I work with Ben Hogan. He's a friend." Most of my fellow LPGA players and all of their caddies and coaches would have laughed like the guard at Seminole.

The second time I went to Seminole as Mr. Hogan's guest, I took Kirk and we got the same reaction. This time we were driving a maroon-and-pink Econoline van. A small step up but not by much. The guard didn't laugh at us this time, but when Kirk walked into the locker room the attendant barely looked at him as he began escorting him toward the small lockers in the back. Along the way, he said, "Who's the member sponsoring you today?"

Kirk said, "Ben Hogan," and four guys sitting in chairs nearby broke into spontaneous laughter. Then the locker room attendant, who was in no mood to be jerked around, snatched Kirk's guest slip out of his hand. When he read the name of the member, he marched Kirk back to the front of the locker room and gave him the best locker along with an offer for anything else he might need.

Word traveled fast. Ten minutes later, when we got to the first tee, between twenty and thirty people were congregated around us. They couldn't see Mr. Hogan, but they wanted to see who on earth he might have sent as guests.

Not only did I not talk much about my relationship with Mr. Hogan out of respect for him, but I knew that he never wanted the publicity that came with helping me or anyone else. When he was helping Tom Byrum, he always told him, "I don't want to read about what I'm telling you here. This is between you and me." He was never that explicit with me, but I also understood that he didn't want to have to answer questions about his protégés, and he sure didn't want people showing up at Shady Oaks asking for lessons.

I was at the Champions Dinner for the 1986 Colonial National Invitational when I found out the 1991 U.S. Women's Open was going to be played at Colonial. I made it my goal to play in it. Mr. Hogan and I talked about it and he knew how important it was to me that I play in that Open. I would ask him if he was going to come out and watch me. He'd say things like "I'll be the one sitting in the bleachers doing this"—and he'd let out a loud whistle. Or, "I wouldn't miss it for the world." I was pretty sure he wouldn't show up, but it was fun banter.

This was the second time the USGA had brought an Open to Colonial Country Club. In 1941 Marvin Leonard enticed the USGA with twenty-five thousand dollars to get the Open on his course. Colonial was only five years old at the time, and the only course in North Texas with bent grass greens. Craig Wood, who also won the 1941 Masters, won that Open, shooting four over par to beat Byron Nelson. Since it was played eight months before the bombing of Pearl Harbor, nobody remembered much about the event, other than the heavy-duty Texas thunderstorms that blew through and suspended play. Fifty years after that first Open, the USGA came back to Colonial with the Women's Open, the first time that premier women's tournament had ever been held in Texas.

It is impossible to figure out how the USGA selects sites for its championships. Sometimes they go to classic courses like Pine Needles in North Carolina or Cherry Hills in Denver, and sometimes they go to new courses like Blackwolf Run in Wisconsin or Old Waverly in Mississippi. Sometimes they pick courses that have hosted a Men's Open, like Atlanta Athletic Club or Oakmont, and sometimes they go places you have trouble finding with an up-to-date GPS, like Prairie Dunes in Kansas. There is a site selection committee, but the process is a bit of a mystery. Just how they settled on Colonial for July of 1991 remains anybody's guess.

. . .

When the 1991 season started I wasn't qualified for the U.S. Open. Unlike a standard full-field tour event where qualified members of the LPGA Tour are eligible to play, the U.S. Open is, as the name implies, "open" to everyone. At the time exemptions were given to players who were in the top forty on the LPGA money list two weeks prior to the Open, meaning that if you had played well enough throughout the year to be among the top forty earners in the women's game, the USGA gave you a place in the field. The rest of the spots are open to anyone, amateur or professional, who earns a spot through a series of qualifying tournaments the USGA hosts around the country. The 18-hole qualifier is a lot of pressure, especially for someone who wanted to play in the Open as badly as I did. Thankfully, I finished second in the LPGA event in Tucson, a finish that not only qualified me for the Dinah Shore, but also put me into the top forty on the money list. The Dinah Shore (now known as the Nabisco), which is the first major of the LPGA season, is comparable to the Masters on the PGA Tour. Everyone knows the layout because it's played on the same course every year—Mission Hills in Rancho Mirage, California—and it is invitation only. At the time, you only got invited if you finished top three in a tournament the two previous years. I was thrilled to be playing in another Open. I had only played in two at that point, one as an amateur, where

I'd missed the cut by one shot, and one as a pro, where I'd finished tied for forty-ninth. Nobody in the field knew Colonial better than I did, so I felt good about my chances. I did wonder, though, if anybody on the site selection committee had been to Texas in July. They don't call those long, hot summer afternoons dog days for nothing. Even the members at Colonial avoided afternoon tee times in July, and the superintendent always had to work hard to keep the bent grass greens from wilting under the oppressive heat and humidity.

Weather and course conditions were far down the list of things on my mind in the weeks leading up to the Open. I spent a lot of time with Mr. Hogan, hitting the kinds of shots I would need to play well in tough conditions. We focused mostly on my driver. He wanted me to feel comfortable hitting both draws and fades, because Colonial requires you to hit it both ways, especially off the tee. The USGA was notorious for taking great golf courses and turning them into virtual torture chambers. Pebble Beach is a fun place to play until the Open comes to town. That week it's so hard you want to quit the game. Colonial was no different. Once the USGA got involved, the course transformed from a wonderful, classic test of golf to a course on which even par might be a miracle.

Of course, the USGA grew the rough high and hardened the fairways. That was to be expected for a national championship, but they also attempted to harden and speed up the greens, which turned out to be a big mistake. Not only is Texas a steam bath in the summer, the winds coming in off the plains can act like a blow-dryer. Hard ground turns to cracked, burned ground and stressed grass turns to dead grass in those conditions. That's what we had to look forward to at Colonial. Plus, members usually continued to play the course right up to the week of the event. It was their golf course and their right to play it as long as they wished, but in the days before soft spikes, the added play roughed up the already thin and stressed greens.

Betsy King, who had won back-to-back Opens before arriving in Fort Worth, was almost brought to tears over the conditions. She said openly that the USGA was trying to embarrass us on national television, and she offered a thousand dollars to any USGA official who could hit a shot within fifteen feet on the 9th hole. Others were equally critical, although Betsy got most of the press.

Course conditions also slowed down play. It's hard to play fast when you're avoiding the bumps and bruises on the greens. We played so slow that week that Lori Garbacz ordered a Domino's pizza from a pay phone between the 13th and 14th holes, and it was delivered to her at 16. In front of a laughing and cheering gallery, Lori gave the driver a twenty-dollar tip. It was a creative way to demonstrate how slow the play was, and another embarrassment for the tournament committee. Lori was known for her stunts. Another time she brought attention to slow play by having her caddy carry around a lawn chair and newspaper, which she dramatically used every chance she got.

I have always loved playing in the majors. The courses are tougher and par is always a good score. If you keep making pars, you're usually gaining on the field. Yes, double bogey is lurking on every hole, but if you keep those to a minimum, don't lose your temper or patience, and continue to grind out pars, you have a chance to be in contention on the weekend.

Mr. Hogan seemed excited about my chances. In the weeks leading up to the Open, we had worked on shaping shots with the driver and on visualizing my game plan. We talked about what holes I could attack and which ones I needed to be patient on. During a normal week on the LPGA Tour, a player might go for the pin eight to ten times depending on how soft the greens are and where the flags are cut. In a U.S. Open, if you go for three or four pins in a round, you are living dangerously.

I did what has now become my pre–U.S. Open routine of playing nine holes on Monday of tournament week, and then an early eighteen holes on Tuesday. I finish off my preparation with nine holes again on Wednesday. Too many players get to the majors and wear themselves out by practicing more than they usually do. The U.S. Open is enough of a grind without starting out tired.

On Tuesday, my family and I had dinner with Judy and

Gardner Dickenson, the Hogans and Valerie's sister, Sarah, whom I had gotten to know pretty well because she was a golfer. It was fun to see Mr. Hogan in that setting, relaxed with his old friend. He and Gardner went way back. Gardner had been Mr. Hogan's assistant when he was the head pro at Tamarisk Country Club. I got to know Judy and Gardner my first few years on tour, but we hadn't really talked much about Mr. Hogan. I think he was a little surprised when I invited them to dinner, and he saw how close we were. After that dinner when I would talk to Gardner, he would tell me stories about Mr. Hogan. One of my favorites was how he would slip Mr. Hogan questions from an IQ test and record his answers. Over the years he gave him a pretty thorough test, and said he was one of the smartest people he had ever met. I received a beautiful note from Mrs. Hogan thanking me for a wonderful dinner and telling me how much they enjoyed being with good friends.

I went to Shady Oaks on Wednesday to practice and see Mr. Hogan. I didn't ask him if he was coming out to the tournament, because I didn't want him to feel like he had to. At that point, I wasn't sure I wanted him to. If people recognized him, the scene would get crazy. I knew how difficult it would be for him to get around and manage that attention. Plus, deep down, I wasn't sure I wanted people to know about our friendship. I knew that if people found out about it, there would be too many questions to answer.

My dad was caddying for me that week. He might not be great with yardages but he was the best at staying positive. I could make five bogeys in a row, and Dad still believed I would make birdie on the next hole and he made me believe it too. Mr. Hogan thought I was swinging fine. He preached the mental side of the game, and how important it was in a U.S. Open to remain patient and manage your game around the golf course. He was right on both counts. During the opening round I realized just how tough a week this was going to be. The greens were beaten up by the time we started the first round. They all would have more accurately been called blues instead of greens. I looked at the grass and thought, *These things aren't going to live through the week.*

I didn't score particularly well in the first round, but I didn't shoot myself out of the tournament either. You can't win the U.S. Open in the first round, but you can lose it. My 77 didn't lose it, but it put me well down the leaderboard, eight shots off the lead, held by Pat Bradley.

In a regular LPGA Tour event I would have been worried about the cut after a first-round 77, but I knew that in the U.S. Open the difference between 77 and 69 could be two bad swings, a couple of bounces, and a putt or two. I didn't hit the ball terribly, but I didn't strike it as crisply as I'd expected either. I felt as though I were swinging defensively, trying to stay out of trouble rather than picking a line, staying positive, and hitting the ball to my spot. I had played late and would play early the next day, so I didn't practice much after my first round.

I spoke with Mr. Hogan, and as usual he offered succinct advice. "Survey the situation. Choose your shot and hit it!" he insisted. He always talked about not being afraid of the trouble. "You have to know where it is and then select your shot and trust it," he told me repeatedly. More than anyone, Mr. Hogan understood that golf wasn't a game of chance, especially in a U.S. Open. You had to have a strategy and you had to have considered a spectrum of variables ahead of time before executing that strategy. I don't think he ever played a tournament round where he hadn't thought through every scenario and considered every option. The fact that he probably had a photogenic memory certainly helped with all of these calculations. In a U.S. Open, where one mistake can lead to disaster, Mr. Hogan beat most of the field by having visualized and practiced shots that other players hadn't even considered. We went hole by hole, shot by shot, in our conversation, and he coached me through the mistakes I'd made, and how I could correct them.

I did better on Friday. My putting improved, in part because I had an early tee time and the greens were still relatively smooth. I didn't feel like I made as many mental mistakes in the second round. I closed with a one over par round of 72, but I still didn't feel like I'd hit the ball well, especially given how hard I'd worked on my swing going into the week. So, rather than hang out on the range at Colonial with the other players, coaches, caddies, and fans, Dad and I got in the car and rode out to Shady Oaks.

I stopped by the men's grill to let Mr. Hogan know I was going out to practice and to let him know it was my dad with me. I got a drink and then went out to my favorite spot on the Little Nine. I had been hitting for about five minutes when he showed up. After a few pleasantries with Dad we got down to business. It only took a couple of swings for him to realize what I needed to do. "You're leading with your head," he said. He demonstrated by taking a mock backswing and then sliding his head forward before the club ever moved on the downswing. Then he showed me how that forced me to cast the club from the top and work my head and shoulders up to make contact. The result was a weak cut or pull. It was a problem I'd had in my swing for a long time, and one that increased under pressure.

"You can't start the downswing with your head and arms," he said. "You've got to start with your hips and legs and then hit it." It was a theme I knew well.

We worked on this for a while. I had given my dad strict instructions to sit quietly in the cart. But he couldn't help himself. He got up, took a step forward, and said, "Don't you think she's taking it a little outside in her backswing?"

Mr. Hogan didn't even look at Dad. He just pointed his thumb in his direction and said to me, "Who's this idiot?"

We all laughed. Apparently, my dad is as hard to offend as I am.

It turned out Dad was right about the symptom, just not the cause. I was taking the club slightly outside the plane line at the start of my backswing, but that was the result of having my shoulders open and not having enough tilt in my spine angle. Again, it was like I was standing straight up and trying to toss the ball down the fairway instead of setting up in a position to make a good, aggressive swing. We talked about having the proper sequence in the downswing, meaning I should lead with my hips and leg, leaving my arms, shoulders, and head to follow. As a doctor, Dad understood that recognizing a symptom is not the same as diagnosing the disease, so he kept quiet and let Mr. Hogan work through the trouble spots with me until I felt comfortable with the sequence and was able to start my ball on line with crisp strikes.

I left Shady Oaks feeling good about what we had worked on, and I was excited for the next day. I just had to transport all of that knowledge the six and a half miles from the Little Nine at Shady Oaks to the first tee at Colonial. I started the weekend tied for twenty-fourth, and I had plenty of company. Twelve players had the same thirty-six-hole total as I had. Any of us could have made a move. That was what happened on Saturdays in majors. Players came out of nowhere to move up the leaderboard, and those among them who weren't accustomed to seeing their names in the headlines fell away.

My hope was that I could implement what Mr. Hogan and I had worked on the previous afternoon. From the opening tee shot, I could sense that this was going to be a better day. I was trusting my swing. Rather than having to fight to find the fairways, I was able to pick a line, relax, and hit it. Because of the thirty-six-hole cut, there weren't as many players in front of us on the weekend, so the greens, while still bumpy, weren't as dinged up as they had been in the first two rounds. A well-struck putt would hold its line.

I made a couple of birdies, and Mom was going crazy in the gallery. She was a loud, nervous fan, and I loved it. My dad kept saying, "Nice shot," as I hit one fairway after another. I can't say it seemed effortless—no U.S. Open round is easy—but the subtle changes Mr. Hogan and I had made to my setup, and the conscious effort to start my downswing with my hips and legs while keeping my head back made a world of difference.

I got up and down out of the greenside bunker on 18. I knew I'd played well, but I wasn't exactly sure what I'd shot. That happens a lot when you're having a good round: You get so into the moment that you lose track of your overall score. It wasn't until my dad told me I'd shot 67 and the people in the scorer's trailer began to congratulate me that I grasped what I'd done. My 67 was not only the low round of the tournament, it was a single-round U.S. Women's Open record.

Just like that, I'd vaulted into a tie for fifth place with Meg Mallon and Chris Johnson, just two shots behind the leaders, Pat Bradley and Joan Pitcock. Amy Alcott and Brandie Burton were both one shot out of the lead, which meant I would be the third-to-last group out in the final round, paired with Chris Johnson, a perfect spot to mount a winning charge.

I called Mr. Hogan and he was thrilled. "That's more like it," he said. "Stick with that through tomorrow, now."

I slept well on Saturday night, far enough from the lead not to let too many pressure-filled thoughts enter my brain, but close enough to know that this could be my time. Colonial had a Wall of Champions by the first tee, a board listing all the tour winners from the events held at this storied course. Mr. Hogan's name was on it five times. I wanted my name on that wall along with his.

Sunday was what a July day in Texas is expected to be, so hot the armadillos get heat stroke, with a westerly breeze that felt like steam rising from a kettle. I was used to the heat, so I thought it might give me an advantage. I felt good on the practice tee and was surprised and pleased when I headed to the putting green and saw Terry and Malanie Crouch, our longtime pro from South Dakota and his wife. They had made the trip down with another family friend, Ray Laird. He played regularly with my dad and I had been playing with Ray when I broke 80 for the first time as a kid. The three of them had driven all night to be there with me. Seeing them raised all kinds of emotions in me, not the least of which was determination. I didn't want their trip to have been in vain.

As we headed to the first tee, I'm not sure who was more excited, me or Dad. I had huge support in the gallery. Mom was there cheering louder than anyone else along with both of my brothers. At one point, Mike pulled me aside and looking me in the eye said, "You can do this." It meant a lot coming from him. He was a great player who had had a lot of success in his own right.

I hit the ball well through thirteen holes but hadn't made any putts, my Achilles' heel. If Mr. Hogan had actually said that I would struggle as a pro because of my putting, he hadn't done it to be mean. He knew from experience how that felt. Once his eyesight went, he had trouble reading the most obvious of breaks, and became afflicted with a form of the yips. I'm not sure he knew there was a word for it, but he once told me that there were times he stood there, frozen, not being able to move the putter. "Once I got it back, I could follow through. I just couldn't take it back!" he told me with utter disbelief. "I could hear murmurs from the gallery." He felt the only way to solve the problem was to play through it and he played with the yips for a while before he finally stepped out of the spotlight.

I always putted well in streaks, but the streaks were never long enough or consistent enough, no matter how well I struck the ball. This was one of those rounds. I was one over par for the day and two strokes behind Meg. If I'd made any putts, I would have been leading the tournament. Instead, I looked at the board and knew that I needed to make birdies. Then I heard the roar of Meg's birdie coming from the 14th green. That sealed it. Pars would no longer do.

It is never a good idea to press in an Open. I started going for pins I had no business going for and taking too many chances, all the things Mr. Hogan had cautioned me against.

I watched the leaderboard and saw that my U.S. Open record had lasted all of twenty-four hours. Beth Daniel shot a 66 on Sunday to set a new record before my old one could make it into the books. It wouldn't be the shortest U.S. Open record I ever held, however. A few years later, at Pine Needles, I held the all-time scoring record in the U.S. Open for about forty-five minutes until Annika Sörenstam finished, and beat it by six strokes.

This week, though, the only thing that mattered was the low total at the end of Sunday. I foolishly went for the pin on 14 and made bogey. At 15, I didn't put my drive in good position but went for the pin anyway. The result was an ugly double bogey. Just like that, I had gone from two shots out of the lead to being seven back. My dream of getting my name on the wall with Mr. Hogan was shattered. At least I went out fighting, but that didn't make me feel any better at the time.

Mrs. Hogan would tell me later that Mr. Hogan, watching at home, agonized over my troubles. When he realized I was out of contention, he decided to make the trip out to Colonial. Not wanting to draw attention away from me, he wouldn't have come if I had a good day, but he knew that I would be disappointed so he wanted to be there for me.

Mrs. Hogan worried about what he would encounter at Colonial. She also knew he felt he had to be there, and there would be no talking him out of it. Five minutes later, as I was struggling to regain my footing and get back on the par train, Mr. and Mrs. Hogan, along with Sarah Harriman, were in his Cadillac, heading to the course he knew better than anyone.

I didn't know how long he'd been there when I saw him from the 16th green. I remember feeling shocked and pleased to see him, and also a bit nervous for him, all at the same time. He had not attracted any attention, in part because very few people recognized him. He had on big wire-frame glasses and he wasn't wearing his traditional front-clipped hat, so he looked like the countless other older men in the gallery. I would have thought that more fans of the game would recognize what they were seeing, but I guess it was like seeing a

famous former movie star in a restaurant. You think you recognize them, but your mind can't quite make the connection.
Of course, eight years earlier I hadn't been sure I would recognize him at Shady Oaks either.

I walked over and gave him a quick hug as I was walking
from 16 to 17. I didn't make a big deal of speaking to him,
but my dad, standing on the 17th tee, turned to the other
caddy in our group and said, "See that old guy in the straw hat
over there?"

The other caddy scanned the gallery and nodded.

"That's Ben Hogan," Dad said.

The caddy snickered and said, "Yeah, right."

"No, it really is," Dad said, but the other caddy didn't
believe him, so my dad quit trying to convince him.

Mr. Hogan didn't try to hide, nor did he make a point of
being front-and-center. If anyone had known he was coming
ahead of time, it would have been as big a story as the winner
of the tournament, which was exactly what he didn't want. It
helped that nobody knew about our friendship. Even if someone had recognized him, the natural thought process would
have been *Hey, that looks like Ben Hogan. No, it can't be. Why
would Ben Hogan be out here following Kris Tschetter?* Even the
other players didn't know that he was there and didn't recognize him if they saw him.

On the final hole, I finished with a par to shoot 76, nine
shots worse than the previous day and ten more than I needed

to win the tournament outright. Meg had shot a 67 of her own on Sunday to break away and win by two over Pat Bradley.

After I signed my card, I walked out of the scoring tent and saw Mr. Hogan standing there with everyone else. He hadn't wanted any special treatment. He was a fan like all the others. I walked up, wrapped my arms around him, and whispered, "I wish I'd played better today."

"I know."

"I wanted to get my name up on that wall with yours."

"I know; you'll be there, someday."

I was trying hard not to cry and just barely succeeding.

"I'm glad you came out today."

"I wouldn't have missed it."

He understood my disappointment better than anyone.

We talked a little more and, as usual, he got me laughing. There is a great picture of us taken at that moment, but for the life of me I can't remember what he said. People had figured out who he was and why he was there. The press was closing in. Mrs. Hogan made an excuse about getting him somewhere cooler, and they disappeared.

It was the last round of professional golf Mr. Hogan witnessed in person, and a moment I will cherish for the rest of my life. It wasn't just the fact that it was the U.S. Open, the tournament he owned like no one else. It was that he had come out to see me knowing what he might encounter the prospect of being recognized and mobbed. It was more important for him to be there for me on a bad day, and that meant more to me than he would ever know. It is a time I remember sweetly, and somewhat sadly. Our daily routine would soon be a thing of the past, as we each moved into different stages of our lives, into the beginning of a long good-bye.

"YOU CAN ADD AN LPGA
VICTORY TO YOUR LIST."

Change is inevitable and there were many changes coming for both me and Mr. Hogan. Life took me away from Fort Worth much of the time in the nineties. I was traveling thirty to thirty-five weeks a year on tour and spending a lot of time with Kirk, whom I would marry in 1997. He lived in northern Virginia near Washington, D.C., and by 1993 I was spending more time in Virginia than I was in Fort Worth. Kirk is a teaching pro and he is one of the best I've ever worked with. I had several teachers during the time I was at Shady Oaks, but Mr. Hogan had been my main teacher. When I met Kirk he took over that job. Unlike so many teachers, he understands that everyone has limitations that cause them to compensate in their swing. He tailors his teaching approach to each student and he continues to learn and grow and become a better teacher each day.

I continued going out to Shady Oaks when I was in town, but those times were becoming few and far between, and when I wasn't there, Mr. Hogan wasn't practicing.

I had been noticing for years that Mr. Hogan's memory was slipping. He would tell me stories that he had told me before or he would say something that just didn't quite make sense, like the time he wanted me to see his shoemaker. He was always trying to help me in any way he could. I had been complaining about my aching feet when he said, "Let me get you set up with my shoemaker in New York. He is the best. He made all my shoes when I was playing on tour."

"Uh, Mr. Hogan, do you think he's still in business?"

"Well, I don't know. Why wouldn't he be?"

"Wasn't that about twenty-five years ago?" I said.

"Hmm. I guess it was." We laughed about it, but now, looking back, maybe that was the beginning of his confusion.

In the winter of 1991, I played in the J.C. Penney Classic with Billy Andrade, a mixed-team event with players from the PGA and LPGA Tours. We were tied for the lead with Hollis Stacy and Gene Sauers going into the final round, and one shot ahead of Ed Humenik and Elaine Crosby and the defending champs, Davis Love and Beth Daniel. I was a nervous wreck going into that final round, so I called Mr. Hogan on Saturday night. At first he seemed a little confused about who I was. (He was never as sharp later in the day.) Once we started talking about golf, though, his mind cleared. He calmed my nerves by telling me to focus on each shot.

"Map out the round in your mind ahead of time," he said. "Once you know what shots you're going to hit in a round and that you've hit those shots before in practice, you'll calm down and be fine."

I did what he said, but I was still nervous. Thankfully my partner, Billy, who had been a good friend since our days playing junior golf together, was the perfect cheerleader. He and Boo, his caddy, kept me calm and focused and thinking positively throughout the round.

Billy and I had gone seventy-one holes without a bogey when I was left with a five-footer for par on our 72nd hole, to get us into a play-off. It was the stuff that dreams are made of. My dad was caddying, my mom was in the gallery, and I was playing with a great friend. You always make them in your dreams, and I made this one. It was the biggest crowd I'd ever played in front of and they went wild. It was a great feeling, but it had only gotten us into the play-off. We still had our work cut out for us.

The play-off started on 16, probably the hardest hole on the golf course. It is a slight dogleg right with water all down the right side and trees on the left. We were playing an alternate-shot format in which everyone hit a drive and then hit their second shot from their partner's drive, then chose the best one and alternated from there. I remember thinking, *Just make sure you get your drive in play. You don't want to be standing alone out in the fairway,* meaning I wanted us to have two chances for our second shot. We both drove it in play, but Billy missed his second shot way right. The pin was cut back-right, which would have left us with a difficult pitch over a bunker, and it looked like Elaine and Ed had hit it close. I had 155 yards, which put me in between clubs. Not exactly the scenario I was looking for. Mr. Hogan had always taught me to play away from the trouble, but I determined that the right bunker wouldn't be too bad. He also taught me that one way to take a little off a shot was to hit a fade. The hole just looked like it called for that shot. I remembered him telling me to put myself on the golf course when I was practicing and then make it feel like practice when I was playing. I put myself on the Little Nine, hitting a fade into my favorite oak tree. The result was a perfect little cut with my 6-iron to about fifteen feet. Billy hit a great putt that looked good all the way until it slid by on the left edge. Ed had also missed, so we headed to the par-3 17th.

On par-3s you started alternating after only one shot. The hole played long for the guys, but Billy, probably hitting a 2-iron, nailed it to about twenty feet. I thought I'd made the putt, but we had to settle for a tap-in par. Ed left his putt about six feet short, and when Elaine missed, Billy and I had won. Mr. Hogan, watching the event on the television in the men's grill at Shady Oaks, yelled, "Did she win it?"

We had played seventy-four holes without a bogey. It was an unofficial event, not one that counted toward the money title or player-of-the-year honors. However, it was the biggest money tournament I had ever played in, and the pressure, having never won in my four years on tour to that point, was huge.

When I called Mr. Hogan after signing my card and spending some time with the media and sponsors, my first words were "I won!"

He said, "I'm delighted for you."

I told him he had helped me more than anyone, and I didn't care what he said. I owed him more than I could ever repay. Of course, he disagreed.

After I hung up with him, some friends from Shady Oaks called to tell me how excited everyone was. The club championship was going on, but everyone had been in the grill watching the play-off. They told me Mr. Hogan was so cute and that he had been more excited than anyone.

My second win came not quite a year later at the 1992 Northgate Computer Classic in Minnesota, 250 miles from where I grew up in Sioux Falls. It was like a home game for me, with friends and family littering the gallery all week.

Again, I was nervous, but I put together back-to-back rounds of 69 to lead by a shot over Deb Richard going into Sunday's final. It had been windy all week, with Sunday being the worst of all. I called Mr. Hogan on Saturday after I played. He told me to go to the range and practice hitting three-quarter shots into the wind. We also talked about using the wind to hit the ball straighter.

"If you have a right-to-left wind, hit a fade so the ball goes straighter. Use the wind. You'll have much more control that way. It's going to be windy again tomorrow. Stay patient out there," he said.

The winds gusted up to thirty miles per hour on Sunday. I hit it all over the golf course, making seven bogeys, four birdies, and an eagle, but everyone else struggled as well. I birdied four of the five par-3s, hitting two of my shots to within inches of the cup. I made a three-footer for par on the final green to win by three shots.

What could be better? Again, my dad was caddying for me. He came home to a sign in his office that read: KRIS TSCHETTER'S CADDY WORKS HERE. I had friends and family everywhere (all trying to keep Mom calm), and it was the first time my family had met Kirk.

After I signed my card, but before I went to the pressroom, I called the Hogans. Mrs. Hogan picked up the phone and realized it was long-distance. "Do you have good news?"

was the way she answered the phone, and I did indeed have good news.

"Oh, Kris, we're so happy for you. I know you want to talk to Ben. Here he is."

"You can add an LPGA victory to your list," I said.

He laughed. "It's about time," he teased.

I asked him if he had been practicing. When he said he wasn't, I told him I was going to come home and kick him in the coola-kwachy. He said he needed it because he was getting lazy. "Now you're on a roll," he said. "There'll be many more."

One of the strongest things about my mental game was that even when the scores didn't show it, I still felt that I played better than my fellow competitors. My brother Mike is ten times the player I am, but I don't think he ever felt like he belonged out on tour, even though I know he would have been successful if he had gotten his tour card. He was a great ball striker but could get a little wild under pressure. He had fallen on a glass milk bottle as a kid and cut everything in his wrist but the bone. The doctors weren't sure he would ever regain use of his right hand after it happened. I always wondered if that had something to do with his not getting on the PGA tour. He regained use of his hand but always had weakness in his last two fingers. One of which, Mr. Hogan said, was most important in the grip.

Never in a million years did I think I would never win again. I finished second ten times, twice in majors, and had fifty top-ten finishes, but I failed to win another LPGA tournament after that. I'm sure Mr. Hogan was disappointed that I didn't win more, but he never let me see it. He knew how hard this game is. He had lived it, and then lived it again with me. Even though his faculties were failing him, he was always encouraging and loving toward me.

Once Mr. Hogan was no longer involved in his company, the quality of the products he had so diligently perfected went downhill to the point where I could no longer get a set of Hogan clubs that had any consistency at all. This became a real struggle for me. I had played Hogan clubs all my life, and I hated that I was going to have to change. I loved looking down at those beautiful blades. Nothing looked as good as a Hogan iron.

I called Mrs. Hogan to talk to her about it. "I understand, Kris," she said. "I am just so disappointed with what's happened to his company. I'm just so glad he doesn't know. It would kill him."

"I feel like I should talk to him about it, but I don't want to upset him," I said.

We decided that I would change clubs and then hit my Hogans when I was at Shady, where he might see them. It was a difficult decision and yet it was no decision at all. I was a professional golfer and I had to play with good equipment. I changed to Pings. They took a little getting used to but Ping made, and still make, the highest quality clubs around.

Even though I was in town less and less, whenever I was back in Fort Worth, Mr. Hogan and I continued with our same routine. One summer I remember deciding it was time to take a few tournaments off because I had a bad case of the shanks. It is the only time I can remember specifically asking Mr. Hogan to come out and help me. If you don't know what the shanks are, skip the next page, because you don't want to know!

As soon as I got to Shady Oaks I stuck my head into the men's grill to get his attention. He came out and asked me what was going on.

"I see your scores haven't been so good. What's been the problem?" he asked.

"Mr. Hogan," I began, "I really need you to come out today. I need some help. I've got the shanks."

"The what?" he asked.

"The shanks." He was looking at me as if he didn't understand. "The shanks. You know, when you hit it off the hosel and it goes dead right."

"Hmm" was all he said. "I'll change my clothes and be out in a few minutes."

Of course, the first few I hit for Mr. Hogan were good. It always happens that way.

"Those look fine," he said.

Then I hit it. The dreaded low right shot.

"Oh, good God," he said. It was like he had never seen a shank before, or hit one for that matter!

I wish I could say that like Mr. Hogan, I'd never known the problem, but the truth is that once I even shanked it on national TV. I hit the ball and said, "Oh, my God. I shanked it!"

Mary Bryan was the commentator following our group and she said, "Uh-oh. She said the S-word." *Shank* is the S-word in golf. You don't ever want to have to say it.

By the time I got my ball up and down for par, signed my card, and got to my phone, there was a message from my mom saying, "So I heard you said the F-word on TV today. . . ."

Mr. Hogan and I struggled for a while, but he finally figured out that the problem was in my downswing. It was coming too far from the inside and I was getting my weight out on my toes. That put me well out of position, with the hosel headed straight for the ball. The combination of these mistakes caused the dreaded shank. Half an hour later, I wasn't hitting shanks anymore, and we both left the course that day having learned something new. I learned how not to hit a shank, and he learned what a shank looked like.

. . .

I wasn't living in Fort Worth by 1993, but I would try to make it out there every chance I got. Kirk and I had stopped in Fort Worth on our way out to Hawaii one year. We landed and headed out to Shady Oaks to practice. We went to say hello to Mr. Hogan but I could tell he wasn't going to come out unless I was alone, so Kirk and I went out to practice in separate carts.

When he got to where I was practicing, he said, "Are we going to have the sideshow today?" Meaning, was Eric going to be joining us?

"No. I think he's working," I said. I tried to get him to hit but he wouldn't. When it was time to pick up the balls he said, "You rest. I'll go pick them up." I was tired, so I let him. Kirk, hitting balls about a hundred yards away, couldn't believe his eyes. He watched as I sat in the cart while Mr. Hogan picked up my balls. I didn't think anything of it. He did that sometimes because he liked the exercise and I liked the rest. I love to tell people that I'm the only person who has ever had Ben Hogan shag balls for them.

I treasured those times back at Shady Oaks, however brief, and it was tough to hear about things changing while I was away. Mr. Hogan loved Max and Buster, the dogs who had adopted Shady Oaks as their home. Those dogs probably watched him hit more balls than anybody. He would come out of the pro shop, get in his cart, and pat the seat next to him. One or both would jump in and get a front-row seat for a Hogan practice session. Oh, the stories they could have told! They both died while I was away, and I heard that Mr. Hogan cried openly at the loss. Max went first, which was bad enough, but at least he still had Buster. He was a great dog who was always there when Mr. Hogan stepped outside. Buster would wait eagerly while Mr. Hogan got into the golf cart, and then when he patted the seat, he would jump in and nestle right next to him.

When Buster died, the club buried him on the grounds and put a tombstone out beside the putting green. The first time Mr. Hogan came to the club after that, he stopped by the grave, kissed his hand, and touched the stone, spending a last few minutes with his old friend. He really loved that dog.

When I look back on my career I feel immense frustration that I wasn't more successful. Every one of my caddies will tell you that I leave more shots out on the golf course than any other player they know, and like Mr. Hogan predicted it was mainly due to my putting. I just didn't seem to make those putts that could turn your day around. I needed to do what Mrs. Hogan said, "Hit it closer."

On the other hand, though, I played on tour for twenty-three years with a hypermobile body that could have been in

Cirque du Soleil. I had back problems my whole career and then hip problems that went undiagnosed for years. It is hard to separate the physical problems from bad golf, especially when you are in the midst of it. Looking back, I know injuries had quite a bit to do with why I didn't play better, but the bottom line is I didn't do what I wanted to do on the golf course, and it was disappointing to me as well as Mr. Hogan. Oddly, he was always the first person to say there is more to life than golf.

"I'VE TOLD YOU THIS BEFORE, HAVEN'T I?"

The cruelty of dementia and similar diseases is two-pronged. First they rob victims of their minds and their dignity, and then they rip out the hearts of the loved ones surrounding them, one forgotten name and lost memory at a time. As the families and friends of the millions suffering from them will attest, there is nothing more gut-wrenching than watching someone you love experience the stages of these diseases. It is agonizing, merciless, and slow.

In the case of Mr. Hogan, the onset was all too familiar. Beginning around 1992, he would be sitting at his table with the standard crowd and say something like "Looks like the rain's going to blow in late this afternoon." Everyone would agree. Then fifteen minutes later, he would say, "Weather's changing. Looks like the rain's going to blow in late this afternoon."

At first nobody thought much of it. People at that age can forget things. Everyone has had the occasional brain-lock, a momentary lapse where you forget the name of a friend you've known for years or lose the answer to the simplest of questions. It is a common occurrence trait and one we all overlook, especially in the elderly, who have earned the right to be a little more forgetful. It is also not unusual for older people to repeat themselves. There is a comfort in repetition, especially as we age. Many times it's difficult to determine the line between the natural signs of aging and something more serious.

Mr. Hogan's symptoms were also masked by his routine. Consistency is one of the keys to prolonging the well-being of these patients, and Mr. Hogan's unfailing devotion to the same regimen helped him remain functional even after his mind began to falter. His friends knew something wasn't quite right, but nobody wanted to probe. He'd always had his own rhythm and way of doing things, and few found the forgetfulness or confusion alarming.

Mrs. Hogan knew something was wrong. When I would call, which I continued to do regularly, my conversations got longer with her and shorter with him. I remember her telling me he was on a new medication. "It's to help his memory," she said. "I don't know why I'm surprised when he forgets to take it."

Even so, he usually seemed to remember me, perhaps be-cause the first words out of my mouth were always something like "Hey, Mr. Hogan, I'm not on tour this week, so I'll be out practicing every day. Get your coola-kwachy off that chair and come out." Maybe he was just pretending to remember, but as we continued to talk the fog would lift and he would say the right things and ask the right questions.

It didn't matter. Character reveals itself in many different ways, and with Ben Hogan, the mark of the man could be seen in his actions as his mind began to fail him. I've been told that dementia can bring out negative emotions such as anger or impatience, but I never saw that with Mr. Hogan. I saw an added sweetness in his actions and attitudes. He was much quicker to smile and seemed much softer around people. He never got mean.

The first incident where his condition became apparent to all occurred at Shady Oaks. He had driven out to the club for lunch, as usual, and spent a couple of hours in his normal spot. Then he got up, walked out, got in the car, and drove away. Nobody knew where he'd gone. Mrs. Hogan called looking for him, and nobody could find him. Her worry increased with each passing moment as club members and friends put out as many calls as they could without creating a ruckus. Four hours later, he pulled back into his standard parking spot and walked back through the front door of the club as if nothing had happened. When his wife and friends asked him where on earth he had been, he didn't know. He'd driven around for four hours and had no idea where he had gone or what he had done.

That was when everyone knew that he had a problem. That was also when Mrs. Hogan took his driver's license away. His days of driving to the office and the club were over. He would still show up occasionally, but always in the company of his wife or a guardian who was in charge of making sure he was protected. Mrs. Hogan was his chief bodyguard. Not only did she keep the prying press away from him during his final years, she did everything in her power to protect his legacy. She pored over press accounts to see how he was being portrayed. When a biography came out about Mr. Hogan in 1996, she was wounded by the way he was depicted. Not only did the author get a number of facts wrong in her view, she could not believe that anyone would put such salty language in quotation marks and insinuate that her husband had spoken that way.

Her complaints about the book were legitimate. I read some of the book, but couldn't get through it. Too much of it just didn't ring true for me. On the language front, though, I had to chuckle. The words the author accused Mr. Hogan of using were not all that strong, and although I'm certain that he'd used those words and probably others, he was judicious. He spoke differently in the men's locker room or at a gin table than he did when he was out with me or at home with his wife. I doubt he ever swore in front of Mrs. Hogan, her sister, or his nieces. That was what hurt Mrs. Hogan. Even if those words had passed from his lips, they were never meant for public consumption. To have them set out in book form for all to read was more than she could bear. She became furious, going so far as to call the publisher to complain about the things the author had said about a man who could no longer defend himself.

But he wouldn't have defended himself even if he'd been able. He never did. As with every other inaccurate story, he would have let it go, saying, "Won't do any good to say anything. They're going to think what they want to think."

I thought it was a shame that others could not see what I saw in those final years. It confirmed what I already knew. The hard, gruff man was not the real man; that was the act. The real man was the laughing, gentle soul who couldn't wait to ask me what tournaments I was playing in and how my swing was shaping up. He continued to be the kindhearted man who looked across a fairway and saw a dog in a cage and couldn't understand why its owners didn't let it run free, the man whose face would light up like a Texas sunrise when I walked into the room, and the man who never lost his manners even when he lost his memories.

Sometimes I could tell he was a little confused. In those instances I would ask him to tell me a story. He would launch into his favorites: stories about his days caddying at Glen

Garden, and how the big kids would throw his hat out of the caddy yard so he would be busy retrieving it while caddy assignments were given. Finally, he'd had enough. He knew that being the smallest meant being left out if he didn't stand up for himself, so after they had thrown his hat down the hill one too many times, he picked the biggest bruiser in the caddy pen and punched him right in the nose. Selling papers on the street had made him a tough kid and a good fighter. One punch and they never messed with little Benny Hogan again.

He would talk about caddying for sixty-five cents a bag, and how hard he would work to make sure he got two loops in a day. He would remember Marvin Leonard giving him seventy-five dollars to go out and play the tour. His eyes would mist and his voice would quiver as he said, "It was the kindest thing anybody's ever done for me."

After a few minutes of reminiscing like this, he would say, "You know, when I was a young kid caddying out at Glen Garden, a member named Mr. Mayben gave me my first club. I loved it and practiced with it for hours. There was just one problem." He would wait a beat and then say, "It was left-handed!" He would laugh, and I would laugh with him. "It was quite possibly the best gift I ever got and that is why I won my fourth U.S. Open. I had to hit a left-handed shot and was able to do so because Mr. Mayben had given me that left-handed club. I give him credit for that U.S. Open."

When he looked up into my eyes he must have seen the sadness there.

"I've told you this before, haven't I?" he asked.

He'd told that story a hundred times, sometimes repeating it twice in an hour. I smiled and said, "You might have, Mr. Hogan, but it's a great story and I love your stories. Tell me another one."

Some things were just too difficult for him. When his brother Royal died in 1996, Mrs. Hogan didn't tell him right away. For all the rumors that the brothers had had a falling out and that they weren't close, Mr. Hogan always spoke glowingly about his brother. There was genuine love there. You could see it in his face. Royal had loaned Mr. Hogan money when he was struggling on tour, and Mr. Hogan had loaned Royal money later in life when the office supply business hit a slump. There were probably family squabbles—what siblings don't have spats?—but they were brothers who cared for each other.

After a while Mrs. Hogan said, "Ben, I'm afraid your brother Royal has passed away." At first he didn't respond. Then he started crying and stayed slumped in his chair for the rest of the afternoon. Mrs. Hogan never mentioned Royal's passing again, even when Mr. Hogan would ask where his brother was. Why put him through that again?

The last time I saw him, he was lying in a bed in All Saints Hospital in Fort Worth just months before the end. I had moved to Virginia, just outside of Washington, D.C., after marrying Kirk, so my time with Mr. Hogan had been more sporadic than it had been in earlier years. We weren't together every day or even every week, which was a blessing in disguise, really. I didn't have to see the slow decline. There were numerous ailments in the final years, but colon cancer was the toughest. He'd had a large section of his colon removed. Knowing that he was sick, I flew into Fort Worth during an off-week to see him. Both my brothers still lived in town. Eric owned a very successful bar, the Pour House, and Mike played the Hooters and Nationwide tours before becoming a teacher. Flying in to see Mr. Hogan gave me a chance to see my family as well.

I baked chocolate-chip cookies and took a plate to the hospital, where I found Mr. Hogan alone in his room. I'm sure Mrs. Hogan wasn't far away, but when I got there he was resting with his face turned toward the window. "Hey, Mr. Hogan, it's Kris," I said.

His face lit up and he immediately wanted to chat. I told him I was not on tour for a week (in case he'd forgotten that I played golf for a living), I told him about my schedule and my game. We chatted awhile and he seemed to be having a good day. In that final year, as the tournaments he'd won faded into a distant memory, he talked a lot about family and friendships, the people he loved and those who loved him. He remembered how Henry Picard had approached him during the darkest days when his game was, in his words, "awful," and said, "Look, Ben, I don't know what your finances are, but if you need any help, you know you can always come to me." That moment stuck with him much longer than any memory of winning a tournament.

I left the cookies, hugged him, told him I loved him, and that I would see him again soon. But I wouldn't see him again. That visit turned out to be another of life's lasts: the last time I saw my friend Mr. Hogan.

I wasn't around much in those last few years. In addition to living thirteen hundred miles away, I was traveling thirty weeks a year. While I wish I could have been there more for Mrs. Hogan, I'm thankful that I was spared the agony of seeing him go downhill, and lucky that I never got the blank stare of a stranger. How fitting it is that the last memory I have of him is of the two of us chatting as usual about everything and nothing.

Fairfax, Virginia, can be hot and muggy in late July. Sometimes, because of the high humidity, you might not see blue sky for days. On Friday, July 25, 1997, the sky was especially pretty. It was a clear morning and I was sitting outside on my patio thinking about the things I had to do before the weekend. The LPGA Tour was in Warren, Ohio, for the Giant Eagle Classic, but I was tired and was taking the week off before the du Maurier Classic the following week. At the time, the du Maurier was one of our majors and the biggest women's event on Canadian soil. I didn't normally take off the week before a major, but I had been playing a lot and needed a little break to get recharged and ready for another major run.

My phone rang early, which was a little surprising. Even though I was an early riser, the phone usually remained quiet until after nine o'clock. When I answered it and realized it was my brother Eric, I knew something was wrong. His voice was low and tense, and I remember him saying, "I wanted to tell you before you heard it from anyone else."

Everything after that was a blur. The tears came quickly, and I felt myself sinking in my chair. I'd known the moment was coming eventually. Men in their eighties with cancer do die. But no matter how much I felt like I was prepared for Mr. Hogan's passing, you're never really ready to lose a loved one.

In hindsight I was lucky. I was thirty-two years old before I lost someone really close to me, someone who I would mourn. I was probably closer to Mr. Hogan than I was to my grandparents.

Because I wasn't living in Fort Worth anymore, his death did not change the fabric of my day-to-day life the way it would have if he had passed a decade earlier. But he had changed the direction of my life. He had given me the confidence and knowledge to transition from college to the LPGA

Tour, and he'd provided the support and encouragement I needed to press ahead in my career and my life. He had given me so much, and once he was gone I missed him more than I could have ever imagined.

I hung up the phone and stared at the beautiful sky. How could it be so pretty? Shouldn't it be raining?

Then the phone rang again. It was a woman reporter. She wanted to know if I would like to comment on Mr. Hogan's passing. I don't even know why I answered the phone. I was sobbing and couldn't speak. This stunned her. She said, "I'm sorry, I didn't realize you were that close to him."

Nobody outside my family knew how close we were or how much he meant to me. He had been kind and generous to me, and he had taught me so much. No matter what my problem, he was always there for me. He was a surrogate grandfather, but he was much more. He was my teacher, mentor, confidant, and friend.

For the next couple of days I went through the motions with a knot in my stomach. I booked a flight to Fort Worth before I knew the details of the funeral. I didn't think about the protocol. It was one thing to go to a funeral for a friend or relative, but when that friend was also a legend, the logistics got a little more complicated. It didn't dawn on me until I was standing outside the church that I might not get in, let alone find a place to sit.

He had passed early that Friday morning in All Saints

Hospital with Mrs. Hogan by his side. I was later told that she had called Tex Moncrief, a local oilman and former president of Shady Oaks. After George Coleman passed away, Mr. Hogan had made Tex the executor of his and Mrs. Hogan's estate. A crusty old Fort Worth native who didn't like small talk or small people, Tex became the traffic cop for information and procedures. He made sure Mrs. Hogan's wishes were followed to the letter, and did so with iron-fisted diplomacy. This was a guy who was the bookie for all the football betting at Shady Oaks in the seventies and eighties, a man who would win and lose thousands at the gin table, and millions in oil deals. He might not be the guy you wanted planning your wedding, but when it came to running interference in a time of grief, nobody was better.

The service was at the University Christian Church, a small church Mr. Hogan attended. We were standing outside when Gene Smyers, one of my friends from Shady Oaks, saw me and took Kirk and me up front. The place was packed. I saw Ben Crenshaw near the front. Sam Snead was one of the honorary pallbearers along with Shady Oaks pro Mike Wright. John Mahaffey and Eddie Merrins, the "Little Pro" from Bel Air Country Club, along with Tommy Bolt and PGA Tour commissioner Tim Finchem, also sat near the front. I didn't see Byron and Peggy Nelson, but I learned that they sat farther back. Mr. Smyers led us to the front section, where velvet ribbons had been placed on the pews for family. I started to object, but everyone sitting in that section insisted that it was where I should be.

Minister Charles Sanders read a moving passage from the Book of Romans, Chapter 5:

Therefore, since we have been justified through faith, we have peace with God through our Lord Jesus Christ, through whom we have gained access by faith into this grace in which we now stand. And we rejoice in the hope of the glory of God. Not only so, but we also rejoice in our sufferings, because we know that suffering produces perseverance; perseverance, character; and character, hope. And hope does not disappoint us, because God has poured out his love into our hearts by the Holy Spirit, whom he has given us.

I could think of no better words to describe the man I knew. He had suffered and persevered. He overcame the many obstacles he faced in life through the strength of his character with respect for others and for God. I didn't know I had more tears in me, but I found them as the pastor spoke. There were no references to the golfer, only words honoring the man, just as he would have wanted it. It was a dignified tribute to the Mr. Hogan I knew.

We somehow ended up in a car to the cemetery with my

good friend Bob Wynn and Ken Venturi, who was as emotional as I was at the service. He and Mr. Hogan were close friends who played many rounds together over the years. He became one of the best golf broadcasters in the world after his Hall of Fame playing career. He talked the entire trip to the cemetery and I could tell he was sincere in his love for Mr. Hogan. What I didn't know at the time was that Mr. Venturi had lost his wife that same year, so his emotional outpouring was more than understandable. I don't think he knew who I was or why I was there, but it didn't matter. He needed to talk, so we listened.

The burial service didn't last long. I remember Mr. Venturi and I both weeping as the casket was lowered. Then we quietly got back in our cars and drove away to Shady Oaks.

When we got to Shady Oaks, his family had gathered in a private room upstairs and they asked me and Kirk to join them. That's when I talked to Mrs. Hogan for the first time that day. We embraced and she thanked me for being there. Where else would I be? I told her how much I loved Mr. Hogan and how much his presence in my life had meant to me. She was far more composed than I. She told me that he loved me too, and she knew that he had loved working with me.

After expressing our sympathy to the rest of the family we went down to the men's grill, where all his friends were sharing memories. There were stories about the "Hawk" and the

"Wee Ice Mon," stories about Ben Hogan the man and the golfer, and stories about Henny Bogan. We remembered his acts of generosity and his eccentricities. We laughed and cried. A few people went to look at his table, but I didn't need to see it. I just looked out the window at the Little Nine, remembering all those afternoons.

I left for the tournament that night. I thought about skipping it, but in the end, I knew what Mr. Hogan would have said: "Get off your coola-kwachy and get out there and play." I did just what he would have wanted. I played.

AFTERWORD

A lot of people have told me I made a difference in Mr. Hogan's life. I hope so. I think so. At least, I gave him a little entertainment in the last fifteen years of it. They told me he would light up when I drove by on my way to the Little Nine and that he looked forward to our practice sessions.

I gave him something to do in the afternoons until the gang would come back for the late afternoon card games. Plus, ours was a relationship like he had never had before. He didn't have children or grandchildren. He loved his nieces, but we had something unique in common, something we both loved: golf.

I've always enjoyed spending time with older people. They have lived life and gained extraordinary wisdom along the way. They have much to give and much to teach, and yet sometimes, in the rush of our busy lives, that is forgotten. I was talking with an older friend not long ago when he told me that there is a lot of aloneness, even loneliness, in old age. Private worlds become smaller and family is sometimes spread across the country so even if you have a close family, it doesn't mean they are always right there for you. By the time I met Mr. Hogan he had very little family left and most of his friends and peers had passed away.

Against all odds we shared a friendship from which we both benefited. For me, there were so many things I gained and value to this day. He shared his incredible knowledge about golf and life. He taught me what it means to be a true and loyal friend. He picked me up and dusted me off when I needed it and he kicked me in the coola-kwachy when I needed that too. Your true friends are the ones who call you out when you screw up, not the ones telling you what you want to hear. I always knew where I stood with him. That is friendship.

He taught me about perseverance and the importance of a strong work ethic. I learned from his example about giving without needing recognition. No one ever knew the extent of Mr. Hogan's kindness and charity, because he concealed it so well—another Hogan Secret. He was a caring, giving, compassionate man, one I might never have gotten to know had I listened to what people were telling me about him.

For him our friendship was a chance to take the journey

all over again, to practice and dig it out of the dirt one more time. I'm sure he enjoyed my youthful energy and lack of cynicism. I was so naïve and trusting. I mean, I gave a ride to someone who had just asked me for a gun.

We accepted each other for what we were. He was one of the few people who never tried to change me. He never told me I needed to quit chatting and focus harder. He knew I needed to talk my way around the golf course as much as he needed to stay focused the entire time.

Mr. Hogan's aura kept people at a distance. At times he liked that. It protected him from being constantly bothered, but it also insulated him from many possible friendships. We gain different things from every friendship. I have friends from all walks of life and each feeds my soul in a unique and special way. I think he missed out on that, especially late in life. So many times he would be sitting at his table alone because everyone had gone back to work. What was he thinking about? I know he thought about how much the game of golf had changed and how much money the young golfers were playing for. I'm sure he was proud that he had had a part in building the PGA Tour into the success it had become. I'm sure he was proud of many things in his life.

After his passing, it became Mrs. Hogan's mission to preserve Mr. Hogan's legacy. She made sure all of his trophies, medals, memorabilia, clippings, and photographs had a permanent home. In June of 1999, she traveled to Far Hills, New

Jersey, to cut the ribbon at the Ben Hogan Room, a beautiful oval museum that is now a wing of Golf House, the USGA headquarters. It's a perfect tribute. Blue-and-cream carpet with his signature in the middle of the floor leads you to cases filled with reminders of a life greatly lived. His golf shoes are there, along with the 1-iron that he hit into the final green at Merion, as well as photos, scorecards, and his U.S. Open medals, including the fifth one, the Hale America medal that he won in 1942, when the Open was canceled because of World War II. He always considered it his fifth Open medal, and from a distance it does look just like the other four.

Mrs. Hogan worked tirelessly to get that museum open. Less than three weeks later, once her mission was complete, she died quietly in her home at the age of eighty-seven.

I have wonderful memories and a little museum of my own. Much more valuable than any collection of trophies and medals, this museum consists of a heavy practice club Mr. Hogan had made for me, his sand wedge that got me through tour school, a few pictures, and an old videotape.

Awhile back I was going through my old VHS tapes, making sure I didn't throw away anything I wanted to keep, when I ran across a tape of my swings. I wore many different, incredibly ugly, outfits. (What can I say? It was the eighties.) So, I'm watching my swing evolve throughout this tape. My backswing is driving me crazy. I always took it back low and inside. I tried to get Mr. Hogan to help me fix it, but it never bothered him. He once told me, "It's fine. You swing a little like that young kid . . . oh, what's his name? You know . . . that young kid who won the Open."

"Are you talking about Raymond Floyd?" (I hated his backswing too.)

"Yeah. That's him."

"Uh, Mr. Hogan. I think he is the oldest person to ever win the Open," I informed him.

"Really?" He seemed surprised. "Well, that swing won the Open. What matters is where you are here," and he showed me a position just beyond impact.

I watched the old tape, full of all the different times I recorded my swing in college and during my first few years on tour. Eric was manning the camera for me in one sequence when you can see a cart come into view and then pull up beside me. Mr. Hogan gets out, says hello to Ass-n-Elbows, makes a comment about my bright pink pants, then asks me how I'm hitting it. Eric had the presence of mind to let the camera run and I watched about twenty minutes of the sideshow. At one point, Mr. Hogan gets frustrated because I'm hitting my driver too low. He keeps telling me to tee it higher, but I won't tee it as high as he wants. Finally, he grabs a ball, bends over, and tees it up himself. I say, "Okay, but if I go under this . . ."

"You won't go under it! A ball goes farther in the air than it does on the ground. Hit it!" I did, and I hit it well.

I was laughing through the tears as I watched the tape.

He was in one other clip. Kirsten was manning the camera that time, but she was hitting pause after every swing. I sure wish she had let the camera run now, but at the time it never dawned on either one of us.

I had some decent years on tour after Mr. Hogan died. But my loose joints finally caught up with me. I started having hip trouble in 1999 and no one could figure out why. Finally, after seeing several doctors I found Dr. Joseph McCarthy, a hip specialist in Boston. He was the first doctor to tell me that the best MRI of the hip was only 75 percent accurate, and that sometimes a tear can't be seen, even with the most advanced technology. Five arthroscopic surgeries and a left and right hip replacement later, I'm still trying to play this frustrating, amazing, addicting, incredible game. I still feel like I have some good golf in me, but I have other things in my life that take precedence.

Before I had kids the thought of not playing golf on tour was depressing to me. I love the game so much and I love the competition. I couldn't imagine retiring from the game I have spent most of my lifetime attempting to master. When I chose to become a parent I knew my professional life would change, but what I didn't realize was that the changes I would experience would only make me appreciate each round of golf I play in a deeper way. Sure, being on tour with kids has its distractions and challenges, but it has given me clarity about what is, and what is not, worth playing for. It has helped me understand that my love of the game is as much about the relationships I have made along the way as it is the trophies on my shelf.

My first child, Lainey, was born in January of 2003. She was born wise. We have always been amazed by how she just seems to understand the things that can't be taught. She is an incredible kid, my athlete. She loves horses and likes golf. She began traveling with me when she was six weeks old and hasn't stopped since. One day when she was six years old she showed me her thumb where a big piece of skin had been torn up while hitting balls. She asked if she had to stop hitting. I told her that if we taped it up she could keep going. After thinking about it for a second, she held out her hand boldly while I taped the blister. Then she picked up her club and went at it again. I knew that somewhere, Mr. Hogan was smiling. His legacy continues.

My second daughter, Kyra, came in October of 2004. She has an amazing inner light. Her passion is music. She'll hit golf balls every now and then, but she would rather be reading a book, jumping on the trampoline, or playing her guitar. They say our kids get parts of who we are as parents, and I am convinced that though they may not fully realize it, some of the life lessons they will learn are lessons Mr. Hogan taught me. The silver lining that came along with all my surgeries was that I was able to be home with my family, and I always cherished the downtime.

I still wish Mr. Hogan had had the chance to have his perspective changed by children. I'm sure I wouldn't have gotten as much of his time, but I don't think he would have missed playing nearly as much. Kids make their way into your heart and become your number-one passion.

Mr. Hogan didn't watch much golf on TV. It reminded him that he wasn't out there. I am the same way. I remember one day on the Little Nine, I asked him why he wasn't watching the Masters. "I'd rather be out here watching you hit balls," he said. At the time I thought it had more to do with his wanting to be playing in the Masters, but now that I have Lainey and Kyra I believe he may truly have meant what he said.

When I turned thirty-five I had to decide if I wanted to become a Senior member at Shady Oaks. I agonized over it for months. The club had meant so much to me, but I was living in Virginia and I just couldn't justify paying so much for a club I so seldom visited. I sent a letter to the membership committee thanking them for everything, and telling them how much I loved Shady Oaks, but that I had to drop my membership. I was shocked, thrilled, and incredibly humbled when I received a response saying they would not let me drop my membership and would instead deem me an honorary member. It is an honor I will cherish always.

I still have my South Dakota and Texas roots, but I guess I'm part Virginian now, having lived here for more than fifteen years. My husband and I bought a seventy-five-acre tract of land in Warrenton, where we created a practice and teaching facility called the Farm. It is our own version of the Little Nine at Shady Oaks. If there is a shot you need to practice, you can find it. It is a heartfelt connection to a time and place that formed me. It is a connection to the man who made those college years so special, a man who gave more than he took, and never made excuses or felt the need to build himself up. Mr. Hogan knew there was only one judge in our world that mattered. He would wait and let Him decide just what kind of person He thought he had been.

I imagine when Mr. Hogan got to Heaven, God gave him Colonial and Seminole along with the Little Nine at Shady Oaks and told him he was home. I just hope that when I get there, we get the chance to play a few more holes.

ACKNOWLEDGMENTS

❖

The game of golf has shaped my life. It has taken me places and allowed me to do things I never dreamed possible and, most important, it has brought many wonderful people into my life, people who just seem to be there for me when I need them most. Someone once said "it takes a village" and this book is no exception. Many people helped me in so many ways throughout the process of writing this book that my attempt at thanks seems impossible. Still, you must know that without you this work could not have been completed.

To my amazing partner, Kirk: Thank you for supporting me while I followed my dream all these years and for following it with me. I have learned so much from you. Your help with this book has been invaluable.

To my strong and beautiful daughters, Lainey and Kyra:

Thank you for your pure hearts and for coming into my life. I love you both more than you will ever know.

Mom, thank you for thinking everything I wrote was wonderful. You are the most selfless person I know and the best mom in the world. If I am half as good as you, my girls will be lucky.

Dad, thanks for teaching me always to find for the silver lining. You introduced me to the great game of golf and you have always taught me by example.

Mike, you have always been there for me. Eric, you always make me laugh harder than anyone. You are the best brothers ever.

Brooksie, thank you for going out of your way to read every draft. You were always there for me when we walked the fairways together, and you still are.

Sharron, you have helped me in so many ways. You listen and offer gentle advice. Thank you for your wisdom and for your wonderful son.

Muffin, thank you for enlightening me about life's endless possibilities.

Kathy, thank you for your enthusiasm for this book.

Julie, you help me in so many ways, it's hard to know where to begin thanking you. Let's just say, thank you for keeping my head where it needs to be. . . . Or at least trying to!

Meredith, I am so thankful you and Freddy and your many talents came into my life . . . another example of the Angels at work. . . . I don't know what I would have done if you hadn't decided to drop everything and put in the countless hours of helping me better express what I wanted to say.

Mary, Alison, and Brian, thank you for being family and Mary (Mimi), thank you for loving my children as if they were your own. We would be lost without you.

Carrie and Stacey, thanks for all the playdates.

Cathy and Cindy, thanks for making playing on tour even better.

Holly, thanks for helping whenever and wherever. I'm glad you had room on your dance card.

Anne, I'm so glad we found each other. Thanks for . . . everything.

Chantal, thanks for keeping me organized (at least trying to).

Amy and MJ, I knew the minute I met you we would be friends. Thanks for never talking to me about golf.

Bobber, Paula, Chris, Julie, Karrie, Jill, Kathy, and Mimi, thanks for being the true friends who, even though we don't see one another often, pick up right where we left off.

Lane, thank you for believing in me and for always being there for me.

Rob, you are a great friend. Thanks for always having my back.

Ray, thank you for that inspiration right when I needed it.

Mr. Pete, thank you for all you do to help both me and Kirk.

Tom, thanks for helping me on so many of your days off. You have kept me swinging.

Keith, thank you for always figuring out a way to keep me playing. You helped me overcome every challenge.

Heidi, you amaze me. I thank God for our timeless friendship. Thank you for your many edits and for coaching me through the highs and lows.

Steve, thank you for your time and effort in bringing order to all of these stories—not an easy task.

Jessica, I couldn't have asked for a better editor. Thank you for helping me make my vision for this book a reality.

Thank you, my village.

MR. HOGAN'S
MANAGEMENT TALK

"Management is as much a part of the game
as hitting the ball." *

Playing:

- The drive is the most important shot in golf—it sets up the hole.
- Before you play a hole, know where the pin is cut so you can set up your approach.
- Work the ball away from trouble.
- Every shot has a purpose—never hit a lackadaisical shot.
- Play the averages.
- Practice your weak shots and continue to practice what you do well.
- Chart the wind each day.
- Use the wind to hit the ball straighter—work the ball into the wind.
- Hit the shot that the situation calls for.

Playing a Practice Round:

- Get to know the golf course. Know where you can and can't hit it.
- Choose where you want to hit each drive.
- Putt and hit to where you think the pins will be, not where they are.
- Study each green—know the undulations.
- Study the hole by starting at the green and looking back to the tee.

Playing in Tournaments:

- Never risk a double bogey—take bogey and walk to the next hole.
- Let the other guy make the mistakes.
- Only take chances when behind.
- Only take chances when the lie is good.
- At night, think over what you did right and what you did wrong.
- Figure out where you can save shots.
- Practice the shots that cost you.
- After you've prepared, the tournament is over—all you have to do is play.

* *"Great comes from outworking them, outthinking them, and outplaying them."*

—BEN HOGAN

ABOUT THE AUTHORS

Kris Tschetter is an American golfer, currently playing on the LPGA Tour. Tschetter turned pro in 1988, having graduated from Texas Christian University in 1987, where she was a three-time member of the All-Southwest Conference Team. As an amateur, Tschetter won the 1983 American Junior Golf Association Tournament of Champions and was a four-time winner of the South Dakota State Women's Amateur Championship (1983–86). In 1984, she qualified for the U.S. Women's Open and the following year was a quarterfinalist at the Trans-National. She founded the Kris Tschetter Celebrity Golf Benefit for Kids in 1991, an event that raises money for children's charities in the Sioux Falls, South Dakota, area. She lives in Virginia.

Steve Eubanks is a former college golfer and PGA club pro and is the author of thirty books, including *Hot Laps, Playing by the Rules, An Afternoon with Arnie,* and *Augusta: Home of the Masters.* He currently resides in Peachtree City, Georgia.